FOUL DEEDS & SUSPICIOUS DEATHS AROUND BRIGHTON

FOUL DEEDS AND SUSPICIOUS DEATHS Series

Foul Deeds and Suspicious Deaths series explores in detail crimes of passion, brutal murders, grisly deeds and foul misdemeanours. From Victorian street crime, to more modern murder where passion, jealousy, or social deprivation brought unexpected violence to those involved. From mysterious death to murder and manslaughter, the books are a fascinating insight into not only those whose lives are forever captured by the suffering they endured, but also into the society that moulded and shaped their lives. Each book takes you on a journey into the darker and unknown side of the area.

Other titles in the series

Foul Deeds and Suspicious Deaths in Blackburn & Hyndburn, Steve Greenhalgh
ISBN: 1-903425-18-2
160pp. Illustrated. £9.99

Foul Deeds and Suspicious Deaths in and around Chesterfield, Geoffrey Sadler
ISBN: 1-903425-30-1
160pp. Illustrated. £9.99

Foul Deeds and Suspicious Deaths in & around Durham, Maureen Anderson
ISBN: 1-903425-46-8
176pp. Illustrated. £9.99

Foul Deeds and Suspicious Deaths in and around Halifax, Stephen Wade
ISBN: 1-903425-45-X
176pp. Illustrated. £9.99

Foul Deeds and Suspicious Deaths in Leeds, David Goodman
ISBN: 1-903425-08-5
176pp. Illustrated. £9.99

Foul Deeds and Suspicious Deaths in Newcastle, Maureen Anderson
ISBN: 1-903425-34-4
176pp. Illustrated. £ 9.99

Foul Deeds and Suspicious Deaths in Nottingham, Kevin Turton
ISBN: 1-903425-35-2
176pp. Illustrated. £9.99

Foul Deeds and Suspicious Deaths around Pontefract and Castleford, Keith Henson
ISBN: 1-903425-54-9
176pp. Illustrated. £ 9.99

Foul Deeds and Suspicious Deaths in and around Rotherham, Kevin Turton
ISBN: 1-903425-27-1
160pp. Illustrated. £9.99

Foul Deeds and Suspicious Deaths Around the Tees, Maureen Anderson
ISBN: 1-903425-26-3
176pp. Illustrated. £9.99

More Foul Deeds and Suspicious Deaths in Wakefield, Kate Taylor
ISBN: 1-903425-48-4
176pp. Illustrated. £9.99

Foul Deeds and Suspicious Deaths in York, Keith Henson
ISBN: 1-903425-33-6
176pp. Illustrated. £9.99

Foul Deeds and Suspicious Deaths on the Yorkshire Coast, Alan Whitworth
ISBN: 1-903425-01-8
192pp. Illustrated. £9.99

Please contact us via any of the methods below for more information or a catalogue.
WHARNCLIFFE BOOKS
47 Church Street – Barnsley – South Yorkshire – S70 2AS
Tel: 01226 734555 – 734222 Fax: 01226 734438
E-mail: enquiries@pen-and-sword.co.uk – Website: www.wharncliffebooks.co.uk

Foul Deeds & Suspicious Deaths Around

BRIGHTON

DOUGLAS d'ENNO

Series Editor
Brian Elliott

Wharncliffe Books

*For Little Edith
In Remembrance*

**First Published in Great Britain in 2004 by
Wharncliffe Books**
an imprint of
**Pen and Sword Books Ltd.
47 Church Street
Barnsley
South Yorkshire
S70 2AS**

Copyright © Douglas d'Enno 2004

ISBN: 1-903425-62-X

The right of Douglas d'Enno to be identified as Author of
this Work has been asserted by him in accordance with the
Copyright, Designs and Patents Act 1988.

A CIP catalogue record for this book is available from the
British Library.

Typeset in 10/12pt Plantin by Mac Style Ltd, Scarborough.

Printed and bound in England by
CPI UK.

Pen and Sword Books Ltd incorporates the Imprints of
Pen & Sword Aviation, Pen & Sword Maritime,
Pen & Sword Military, Wharncliffe Local History,
Pen & Sword Select, Pen and Sword Military Classics
and Leo Cooper.

For a complete list of Pen & Sword titles please contact
PEN & SWORD BOOKS LIMITED
47 Church Street
Barnsley
South Yorkshire
S70 2BR
England
E-mail: enquiries@pen-and-sword.co.uk
Website: www.pen-and-sword.co.uk

Contents

Preface

This volume on heinous crimes in the Brighton area was produced to ensure the 'Queen of Slaughtering-places' is firmly represented in Wharncliffe's growing 'Foul Deeds' series.

An unexpected finding made during its compilation was that it additionally filled a gap in local literature, despite the appearance of a number of murder series over the years in the local press and the publication of several volumes on murders and other crimes in Sussex. That said, the list of Brighton murders on the internet compiled by Richard Witt (whom I here acknowledge) is the only fairly comprehensive catalogue of such crimes I have found to be publicly available.

This book, therefore, is a first. Not only does it contain accounts of a wide variety of murderous incidents in Brighton, linked by six themes, but the people involved – on both sides of the law – express their thoughts and feelings. They come alive in these pages. Local historians and the public will find much to interest them also in the varied range of images included, a number of which have never before been published. In this connection I am deeply indebted to Brighton historian, Chris Horlock, who unstintingly provided me with rarities from his extensive collection.

The book is not in any way intended to be sensational but a record of terrible deeds perpetrated for the most part in our midst. Every murder took place in Brighton except two (in those instances, the victims were worthy citizens of the town). Many will derive interest from the backgrounds to all the cases and find food for thought in the patterns emerging from the extreme violence portrayed. With a five-year-old granddaughter living in Kemp Town, the horror of one case made it difficult for me to remain detached.

Finally, this volume is intended to correct the misinformation in relation to persons, locations and buildings which I have encountered in my researches, although for my part I accept responsibility for any errors that may emerge in these pages.

Acknowlededgments

Special thanks are due to Simon Bradshaw, Editor of *The Argus*, who kindly suggested my name to Rupert Harding, Editorial Director of Wharncliffe Books, as a possible author of this volume. I am greatly indebted to Rupert himself for his guidance, advice and support at all stages of production and also to Brian Elliott, Series Editor. Thanks also to Natalie Clark, Editorial and Production Assistant at Pen and Sword Books Ltd. Others to whom I am grateful are listed below.

Textual Assistance
Alan Barwick, Brian Bidgood, Nina Bouch (Hove Reference Library), David Briffett, Susan Carnochan (Archivist, St Mary's Hall, Brighton), Michelle Collom (Dyke Tavern), Dr Barrie Cook (Department of Coins and Medals, British Museum), Rowan Dore (*The Argus*), George Driscoll; Alison Eyre and Pat Grant (Saltdean Public Library), Stephanie Greene (Brighton & Hove Libraries), Peter Hines (technical/internet support), Stephen Horlock (Brighton Borough Cemeteries), Janet Larkin (Department of Coins and Medals, British Museum), Mike Levy, Jim Marshall, Peter Mercer, Selma Montford, Alan Virgo (Brighton Borough Cemeteries), Mel Peatfield (Cuttings Library, *The Argus*), Greg Perrott, Geoff Wells, Ann Withers (Church Administrator, St John's Church, Preston, Brighton).

Assistance with Images
Bob Ahern (Hulton Archive), Kevin Bacon and colleagues (Brighton History Centre), Philip Bye (East Sussex Record Office), David Beevers (Keeper of Fine Art, Brighton Museum and Libraries), Marc Carlton (Brighton & Hove Hebrew Community), Neal d'Enno, John and Jackie Edwards/Adur Imaging, Getty Images, Esme Evans (Sussex Archaelogical Collections Library), Alan Hayes (Brighton Fishing Museum), Mike Felmore, Danny Howell (Solo Syndication), Robert Jeeves/Step Back in Time, Ken Jones (Chief Constable of Sussex) and Sussex Constabulary, Richard Le Seaux (Keeper of Local History and Archaeology, Brighton Museum and Libraries), Cara Minns (Photographic Library, *The Argus*), Sangita Mistry (Mirror Newspaper Group), Jennifer Nash (East Sussex Record Office), Martin Pittaway (Mirror Newspaper Group), Susan Rowland (for the map in the Griffith chapter), David Shailer, Emma Thackera (Eaglemoss Publications Ltd), Shirley Veater, Jean White (Sussex Archaeological Library, Lewes). Picture credits are shown at the end of each caption.

From 'A New Plan of Brighton and Kemp Town' by Wallis, 1830. Brighton History
Centre

TRUNK MURDERS

CHAPTER 1

Poor Celia Holloway
1831

I asked her to sit down on the stairs and then on the pretence of kissing her I passed a line around her neck and strangled her
(John Holloway)

Just a few hundred yards away from the Royal Pavilion, with its extravagant opulence, once stood the mean dwellings off Edward Street that made up North Steyne Row – familiarly known as Donkey Row. It was to one of these habitations that Celia Holloway, née Bashford, was lured in the summer of 1831 with ghastly consequences.

The dreadful crime committed there earned John Holloway the title of 'Brighton's first trunk murderer'.

One might search Holloway's life and deeds in vain to find any redeeming qualities in the man. Hardly of striking appearance, he yet succeeded in attracting quite a number of women, virtually all of whom he used and discarded. Celia Bashford had the misfortune to meet and marry him. A former employer whose service Celia was in prophetically noted:

I was very sorry when she married John Holloway as I was afraid he would not use her well; and it is well known that he frequently left her and took up with others. She would frequently say to me she would not mind dying under his hands for she always thought she should.

Catherine, one of Celia's two sisters, stated that Holloway 'treated my sister very ill. He almost starved her to death'.

Eleven years older than Holloway, Celia was singularly unprepossessing. With a large head and dwarfish appearance (she stood only 4′ 3″), long arms and hands turned outwards like the paws of a mole, she was not someone Holloway was keen to show off. Physically unappealing she may have been, but in terms of character she was well thought of by others. Her last landlord, James Simmonds, described her as 'a quiet, harmless woman' and his wife 'always had a high opinion of her chastity'.

Exploiting Celia's genuine affection by making her pregnant brought Holloway more than he bargained for – responsibility, or the threat of it. That was something he was unable to handle.

He first met the servant girl from Ardingly at Brighton Races when he was seventeen or eighteen. He wrote later:

> *She was never happy but when with me; but as I did not love her, I only laughed at her folly; and, to tell the truth, I was ashamed to be seen with her until after dark and then to get out of the town and on the hills as soon as possible.*

What do we know of this man?

John William Holloway was born in Lewes on 22 May 1806. Because his father was away at the wars and generally accompanied by his wife, the infant was very soon placed with his grandparents at Litlington, a very small village some seven miles distant in the Cuckmere valley between Alfriston and West Dean. Not until 1815, once Napoleon had been defeated, did John meet his father – in France. Holloway senior returned and was awarded a pension. The reunited family (all three generations) lived in Litlington, where John attended the local dame school. He then went to Alfriston National School and was appointed pupil-teacher at the age of ten or eleven. The minister and senior trustee of Alfriston's chapel later recalled his good qualities.

In around 1818, the family moved to Brighton, a fast-developing town that might offer them better opportunities. Here John's attendance at chapel – first Baptist then Wesleyan – was assiduous, especially on a Sunday. Even on weekdays, he later recalled, time was found for attendance, prayer and reading the scriptures.

Before long, however, a change came over the young man. He later put this down to falling in with bad company and starting to drink. Certainly drink was a factor in his later behaviour. He gave up the chapel and became unreliable in his work. In his relationships with women he was inconstant, selfish and, it transpires, weak-willed. In the case of one Sarah Johnson, for example, he claimed that although he sincerely loved her, his friends persuaded him to give her up. Similarly he was persuaded by his parents to give up Maria Burke, a lodger. Other relationships were doomed to failure. One ended in the girl's unexplained death …

He began indulging in petty theft, stealing a watch and chain from a drunken man sleeping it off in a barn. On another occasion, he convinced a servant-girl to let him guard her trunk and then stole the quarter's wages she had inside when her back was turned.

By the time he was nineteen, however, the law ensured that he took some measure of responsibility for his actions. Although he resisted marriage on learning of Celia's pregnancy, a report was made – presumably by her – to her native parish of Ardingly. Its Overseers refused responsibility for the expected bastard child and placed the young father-to-be in Lewes Gaol until he agreed to look after her and the infant. He was then given an opportunity to rectify matters:

John Holloway in Horsham Gaol, painted at the particular request of his mother by J Perez of Brighton. Brighton History Centre

I was taken up by Ardingly parish. I lay there, to the best of my recollection, five weeks. During this time I received many letters from the parish officers of Ardingly, persuading me to marry. I refused because I had no money; they offered to find money, likewise bail to get me out; I agreed with it; I married through the fear of lying in prison. I did not marry her for love. I have never loved her as a wife; 1 loved her as a friend. I forgot to tell you they did pay all expenses, and bailed me out of prison, and I was married by Ardingly parish, sworn to my own parish, and taken home. My own father and mother did all they could to make us comfortable. I was too young to have a thought of getting a living for my wife and myself. I lived with her until she was confined. During that time we had no angry words between us, but I confess I gave my mind to all kinds of folly.

Back in Brighton, the couple spent a few days in separate wings of the workhouse. Holloway then obtained a temporary gardening job in Dysart Street. They moved into lodgings, first in George Street then in Nelson Street. They did at least have some furniture, bought by Holloway's father – furniture which was later to become a bone of contention.

There were two developments which were to fuel Holloway's resentment of his wife: the first was supposedly learning that the father of her expected child was not him but someone called Edward Goldsmith (Celia always denied this and her husband's word was hardly to be trusted); and the second was the stillbirth of the child, which effectively meant that Holloway had married Celia for nothing.

Moneywise, things went from bad to worse. Holloway found work with a Wesleyan bookseller, William Nute. Charles Hindley, the editor of a volume recounting the Holloway case, explains:

> *... there was a Mr Nute residing at No. 38, Egremont Place, Brighton, a local preacher and agent for the sale of books published in parts, and from whom Holloway had accepted an engagement to procure orders for the same on commission. But he afterwards wrote in one of the many statements made after his committal – 'I tried my utmost to get work, and finding I could not, I took up bookselling for Mr Nute, but that brought in little or nothing, so at last I gave it up.'*

This was unfortunate, since Nute was pleased with his work and was to remain loyal to the young man to the end. This loyalty was not devoid of self-interest, however, since he capitalised on the Holloway case by later producing, with Kelly's of London, a *History of the Brighton Murder, with Life and Trial of Holloway, with fine engravings*, which enjoyed an enormous sale at the time and for some years afterwards. A number of the images from it are reproduced in the present account.

Some welcome income was provided by a lodger, 15-year-old Maria Burke. Almost inevitably, however, she received attention from her landlord and this imposed a further strain on the marriage.

Celia, in desperation, wrote to her brother for money – but most of the fifteen shillings he gave them was spent in a pub by Holloway on his way home from collecting it. A dreadful row ensued some days later when the brother came to the house. Holloway recalled:

> *After she had been confined about three weeks her brother came to our house, and sadly abused me for not getting work, which it was impossible for me to get at that time of the year, which was in the winter.*

The brother returned to Ardingly with Celia, taking the furniture with them. At least he paid for it, giving Holloway £2. Yet this removal of his father's gift only made Holloway more resentful.

Surprisingly, Maria Burke stayed on for a time in the bare rooms until, as noted, he was persuaded by his parents to give her up.

For a time he went away to sea but it says something about his character that he was ordered off a man o'war by the captain, who considered him unsuitable. He came back to Brighton and lived with his parents for a while. He did obtain work as a builder for the brewer George Wigney but was accused of some unspecified dishonesty and was either dismissed or left.

Like a moth drawn to the flame, Celia had by now returned to Brighton. Incredibly, she took up with Holloway again. New lodgings were found in Albion Street and then Circus Street. But the relationship was stormy, Sometimes drunk, he manhandled her and, of course, there were other women.

Despite all that, she became pregnant again. Never home-loving, Holloway (still only twenty-one) took himself off in September 1827 to join the Blockade Service, enrolling under the name Goldsmith, his mother's surname – and the surname of the man he had accused of first making Celia pregnant. For four years, until the Service was disbanded, he served in watch towers on shore, such as at Jury's Gut, east of Camber. He also served at sea, mainly as a painter but also on watch duties, aboard a lugger, *The Badger*, and the brig *Adder*, based at Rye. Encounters with smugglers and other incidents there must have been, but Holloway did not subsequently refer to any.

In Rye there were two fateful encounters, both with women. First, Holloway met a Sarah Sanders. He acknowledged later that he 'did promise to marry her soon after our acquaintance began' but found out 'she was a girl of very bad character.' He could not deal with that:

> *We quarrelled and I was heard to threaten her by a woman of the name of Frost. From that time to the present I have never, to my knowledge, seen her ... But it happened, after I was gone from Rye, that a young woman was found dead, apparently washed on shore; and I think it was said when found that she had a rope around her neck; but the particulars I do not know as I was not there at the time. I only know what I heard when I returned; and I believe it was likewise said that she was in the family way, and her earrings torn out of her ears; and in many other respects her body had the marks of violence on it ... Now after this young woman was found, it was observed that Sarah Sanders was missing and that the last time she*

*was seen was in my company and that she was likewise in the family
way. It was immediately said that the young woman that was found
was the said Sarah Sanders. On hearing of this, Mrs Frost went
forward and stated that she heard me threaten her very much and
that she believed the deceased was the said Sarah Sanders and that
she had not been seen since. On this evidence a warrant was issued
out for my apprehension.*

Although questioned about this incident, Holloway was given an
alibi by his captain. Doubts about the thoroughness of the
investigation, however, were raised a few years later. Yet Holloway
declared: 'God is my witness. I am innocent of that murder.' How
true this claim is will never be known.

The second encounter was with one Ann Kennett who, like
Sarah Sanders, also lived in Rye. Although only about twenty, she
already had two illegitimate children. A real love affair developed,
with Holloway walking the five miles to the town to see Ann
whenever he could in between duty at the watch house.

Holloway, under the name William Goldsmith of the parish of
Winchelsea, bachelor, and Ann Kennett of Rye parish, spinster, were

*Margaret Street stands where the letter N of 'Marine Parade' appears in this close-
up from Wallis's map.* Brighton History Centre

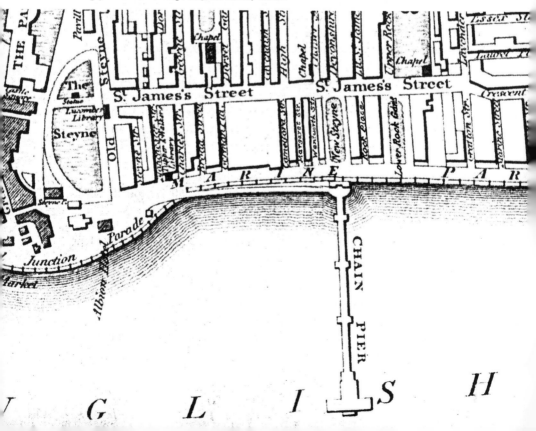

married by licence in Rye parish church on 16 March 1830. With this wedding, history repeated itself: it had been prompted by a pregnancy and a visit from the Overseers (although it might be wondered why Kennett had felt she should bring in the parish officers). Here, too, there was to be no child, for Kennett miscarried.

Holloway's second child by Celia, named Agnes, had meanwhile died in Brighton, aged one. As for Celia herself, times had become hard. She was reliant on the parish, scratching a living selling pins and cotton from a tray. Holloway, however, was to admit that 'he did not care what became of her'.

When Holloway was discharged from the Blockade Service early the following year, the couple returned briefly to Brighton – briefly, because Holloway rightly feared that Celia would be applying to the Overseers for maintenance. There then followed a period of relative prosperity spent as a coiner along the coast east of Brighton but he does not explain how or why this came to an end.

It was back to Brighton again. Holloway, now desperate for work, was fortunate to be taken on by the Royal Chain Pier Company as a painter. In the late spring of 1831, he found lodgings with Kennett in a terraced house at 7 Margaret Street. It was not far from the pier – or from 4 Cavendish Place, where Celia was living with her sister and brother-in-law. Inevitably, Celia applied to the parish officers for maintenance from her husband. The rate initially agreed was two shillings per week, but this level was not kept to. Soon items of food were being provided instead of money. In each case the bearer was, tauntingly, Ann Kennett. Holloway later claimed she was always kind to Celia and occasionally even pawned her clothes to make up the deficit.

On 4 July, when Kennett took round only one shilling, there was a fearful confrontation between the women. Celia angrily exclaimed:

I have nothing to eat. What am I to do with one shilling? I will go to the Overseer to know which John is to keep – his wife or his whore.

She struck Kennett twice with a poker. Kennett seized her and said 'You are too little to hit, but mind, you shall suffer for this'. She left very angry. That evening, Holloway went round to 4 Cavendish Place demanding to know why Celia had gone to the Overseer again. He warned her 'Madam, you think you are going to frighten me but you are mistaken'. He was then so violent that landlord James Simmonds ordered him out of doors. He went out, saying to Celia, 'You damned bitch, you shall suffer for this before many days'.

At this time, she was again pregnant. Holloway suggested that Simmonds was the father, although she had not been living at Cavendish Place at the time of conception. It could feasibly have been Holloway himself on a return visit from Rye. The mystery remains unsolved.

That argument at Celia's lodgings sealed her fate. Holloway was now determined to be rid of her and to clear a way towards accounting for her disappearance began by forbidding her to visit his mother. She apparently complied, and this lent substance to the story which Holloway later put about that Celia had left Brighton for London.

The deed would have to take place somewhere other than Cavendish Place. He spent time the next week looking for a suitable place to rent. He found one in Donkey Row, later to become Sun Street. Its position may be seen above the 'd' of the left-hand mention of Edward Street on Wallis's map (see frontispiece, p. 8).

Ann Kennett as she appeared at Holloway's trial. Drawing by J Perez. Brighton History Centre

It seems unbelievable that Celia was prepared, only ten days after their fearful row and knowing Holloway as she did – and with a baby due in a fortnight – to agree to move to this undisclosed location. Utterly naïve, she clearly believed that this was an opportunity for them to begin a new life together. Perhaps he told her he would give Ann up. It is also astounding that there was not a more searching response from the Simmonds or from the Bishops, Celia's sister and brother-in-law.

On 14 July, Holloway called at Cavendish Place, telling Celia they were going into some temporary lodgings he had found, prior to leaving for London. She had put her clothes in a trunk, which he had come for. He would also take the bed and mattress and come back for her later in the day. Before he left the house, he helped himself to sixpence, which was all she had, in her

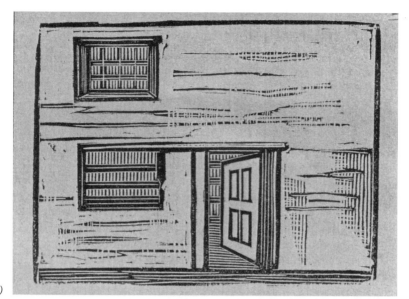

(a) An 'exact resemblance of the exterior' of No 11, Donkey Row, off Edward Street. (b) The interior of the house in Donkey Row where the murder was committed, showing the understair cupboard in which Ann Kennett concealed herself. Inside it, the chaff is on the floor and the victim's head is on the shelf.
Brighton History Centre

workbox. She gave him a penny for a half-pint of beer and went off to buy him a bread pudding at the bakery for his dinner.

Ann Kennett must have known what was afoot, for Holloway would surely have told her what he was planning. He later claimed that, rather than shunning this evil scheme, she was concerned about him getting caught:

> *She said I had better not do it for fear of being discovered. I told her I would trust to that if she would assist me; she said, yes, she would.*

There were, of course, many other options open to her: warning Celia herself or members of her family or friends, alerting the authorities, or even leaving Holloway. He later claimed she was frightened into compliance but this is hard to believe.

Holloway went back for Celia in Cavendish Place. Kennett stayed in 11 Donkey Row, watching and waiting in the silent house, which was completely bare save for the intended victim's trunk, bed and mattress. Like a lamb to the slaughter, Celia walked the short distance from her lodgings with Holloway.

On reaching the southern end of the Row, he told her to wait while he went into the house. He told her a friend of his was sharing the house and he wanted to check whether he was asleep, as he did not wish to waken him. Once inside, Holloway instructed Kennett to wait in the cupboard in the corner of the room:

> *I then went and called Celia. When she was in the house I shut the door, told her I wanted to wait a little while because my partner lived upstairs and he was in bed and we must wait until he got up and with that pretence I kept her in conversation for some time.*

They crossed the brick-floored downstairs room to the open stairway.

> *I asked her to sit down on the stairs and then on the pretence of kissing her I passed a line around her neck and strangled her.*

To implicate Ann Kennett more deeply, he then – highly implausibly – claimed:

> *As soon as I passed the line around her neck, I found it was rather more than I could manage. I called Ann and God knows she assisted me by taking hold of each end of the rope with me and she held the rope with me till the poor girl dropped. I held the cord for a time myself and Ann made use of this expression, 'Do not let your heart fail you.'*
>
> *When I thought she was dead, or nearly dead, I dragged her into a cupboard or coal hole under the stairs and under the stairs there is some nails. I did not remove the cord but took an over-handed knot*

Holloway and Kennett passing the Hare and Hounds, *Preston, on their way to* Lovers' Walk. Brighton History Centre

> *and I made the ends fast to the nails so that she was hanging by the neck.*
>
> *I proposed then cutting her. Ann Kennett told me to wait until the blood settled.*

They meanwhile started a fire in the grate to burn items of clothing which were unlikely to be pawned. Returning to Donkey Row the following morning, Holloway emptied the chaff filling out of the mattress they had brought, as he needed the cover.

Then the mutilation began:

> *I cut off the head first and I think the arms I carried with the head. Ann Kennett was present. I never went to the house to do anything with the body but what I took Ann Kennett with me. And the day that I brought the head and the other parts away, she was to walk behind me to see if any blood came through. The first attempt we made would not do because the blood came through the ticken.[1] Ann told me of it and we went back and put it into a little box and then into the ticken.*

That night they took the head and limbs severed on the brick floor of the downstairs room back to Margaret Street. Letting themselves into the back area, they dropped the grisly contents of

---

1. Fabric used for making a bedtick (a flat four-sided case or cover filled with feathers, straw, or other material to form a bed) or for covering pillows, especially a strong, durable, usually striped, linen or cotton.

the box into the common privy. The rest of the victim was still at
the house in Donkey Row, in the trunk which had held her clothes.

Kennett washed and re-washed the floor, then next day,
giving her name as Ann Goldsmith, went to the pawnshop and
pledged an apron and three gowns. Returning with other
articles later, she said her name was Brown and that she lived in
Carlton Row.

Holloway and Kennett returned to Donkey Row that night.
The trunk was carried out and placed on a wheelbarrow he had
previously borrowed. Holloway went ahead pushing the barrow
while Kennett followed with a shovel and pick. Brighton was
much smaller then and after about a mile they had left the town
behind them and were in Preston Village. Passing the *Hare and
Hounds*, they took the footpath leading to New England Farm
and then crossed a field to a copse near the track known as
Lovers' Walk. This was a popular spot, particularly during the
summer and autumn months of the year.

It was, Holloway recalled, a beautiful night but too dark to dig
a grave. Placing the trunk, pick and shovel under some bushes,
they went back home with the barrow.

At first light, they were back at the site chosen for the burial, a
spot some 150 yards from the high road (writing in 1875,
Hindley stated that it had long since been cut through for the
purpose of making the London and Brighton railway, although a
portion of the copse was still preserved and enclosed within a wall
marking the boundary of the ground belonging to the railway
company). Because of the tangle of tree roots, Holloway could
not dig much of a hole and finally gave up. The torso was
removed from the box and placed in the shallow excavation,
which was immediately filled over with soil. The wooden trunk
was then broken up and the pieces scattered about. That evening,
the couple returned to retrieve the shovel and pick which they
had left hidden under some bushes.

Holloway went back to the site some days later to check the
grave, and visits were made on two other occasions by Ann
Kennett. All appeared to be well.

Yet neighbours in Donkey Row and the surrounding area must
have witnessed all the activity and wondered what it meant and
why it had abruptly stopped. Holloway's story was that Celia had
found work in London as a chambermaid and had taken all her
clothes with her. Even the Simmonds and the Bishops must, for
the time being, have felt their concern was unfounded.

At the end of the week following the murder, the couple moved
away from Margaret Street – but only as far as neighbouring High

The Crown and Anchor *at Preston where the Coroner's inquest was held.*
Illustration by J Perez

Street. Already her lover was straying. One evening she saw him with a prostitute on his arm. She remonstrated with him and he hit her, cutting her forehead.

About this time, the earth at Lovers' Walk was shifted by heavy rain. On 25 July, Daniel Maskell, a fisherman, told his friends that earth in the copse at Lovers' Walk seemed to have been recently disturbed. When he had pulled out a protruding piece of red cotton thread, it had produced a length of cloth. Accompanied by his friend and fellow-fisherman, John Gillam, Maskell returned to the site some days later and they looked at the soil. When they poked it with a stick, it gave out a strong and unpleasant smell. They later told their families and other friends about this but made no report to anybody in authority.

They must have kept thinking about what they had seen, for on the morning of Saturday, 13 August, Gillam, his mother and sister, and a Mrs Sherlock went to inspect the site. They agreed the parish constable, William Elphick, should be called in. Elphick came with a spade and uncovered a bundle of clothing tied with string. Inside was a torso with a male foetus protruding from it.

The dreadful remains were removed to a nearby barn. News of the discovery spread rapidly and thousands of people came to see the body, but only those who paid were allowed to. A contemporary account recorded that:

The copse in Lovers' Walk where some of Celia Holloway's remains were discovered. Brighton History Centre

The Chain Pier, the Devil's Dyke, kept by Mr Peter Berkshire, and all the customary places of resort, were forsaken, and hundreds were seen bending their steps towards the copse, to obtain a view of the unconsecrated grave of the unfortunate Celia.

During Sunday, the little village of Preston was crowded with people visiting the copse and barn where the body was deposited, and hanging about the public house to witness the assembling of the jury and witnesses, and to catch a sight of the prisoners. Indeed so eager were some persons, many of them females, to view the remains of the body after it had been opened, that a hole was made in the barn door, but the effluvia made many of them regret their curiosity. The sister to the deceased, who is said to bear a strange resemblance of her, attracted much attention as she sat, for a considerable time, under the trees in the road opposite the public house.

Visitors searched the fields and hedgerows for the missing head and limbs or any other souvenirs. They even carried off the branches of the tree overhanging the grave and marks were left all around:

On the surrounding trees the name of HOLLOWAY was carved in every direction; himself suspended either on gallows or a gibbet, and in some instances accompanied by epithets too coarse and indecent to be inserted. It is not to be here supposed that the Brighton poets could lose sight of so favourable an opportunity of displaying their poetical abilities. Thus on one tree we read –

Here lay poor Celia. Curses be on Holloway, He'll wish himself away On the great judgment day.

On another – Here lay a wife, a mother, and a child, D–mn him who placed them in a place in so wild.

Even the witling could not allow so grave a subject to escape him without exercising his talent upon it, and thus on one tree we read –

Women are bad – not so was Celia dead; You'll ask me why – Celia wants her head.

Some lace, said to have been part of the cap, was picked up and, with fragments of the gown, was handed about and sold.

Holloway first heard of the discovery of the torso at his place of work:

A person came to me at the Pier, and said that a body was found near Preston, and that the legs and arms were cut off. You may guess my feelings. I thought I should have dropped; but in a few minutes I recovered myself, and began to consider what I had best to do.

However, in a little time I left the Pier, and went home, and told Ann Kennett what was the matter. I had not been home long, before my poor dear mother came up to me. She said, that it was reported that the body that was found had been proved to be the body of poor Celia. She was nearly out of her mind. I bade her be calm, for she might depend upon it it was not Celia; and even if it was, that she might rest assured that I was an innocent person with regard to being the murderer; but I said, Mother, that I will not believe it is her. She then earnestly entreated me to tell her where she was. I said, I do not for certainty know, but have every reason to believe she is alive and doing well. My mother then left me in great distress of mind, because I would not satisfy her where poor Celia was. As soon as I had got rid of my mother, I gave Ann Kennett directions concerning the getting of my wages, and to bring the best part of my clothes to me at Black Rock public-house, about a mile from where I lived; and then I left the house, and went to the place appointed to meet Kennett. I had not waited long, before she came with a bundle of my clothes, and again returned, to get the money due to me at the Pier, and the remainder of my clothes. But when she came back the second time, she told me that it was all a mistake, for it was a young woman that was lost at the races, and the mother and father had been and owned the body : and I concluded in my own breast that it might be so ; yet at the same time it looked very unlikely. But I was resolved to return and go down to my mother's, to learn from her what she had heard about it. But when I got there, she told me that she knew nothing about it, only that it was a young woman. We left there again; but we wanted to take something with us that we had forgotten. Ann Kennett was to go round to our lodgings and get it, and then was to come to me in Chapel-street. But when she got there, some officers were at the house waiting to take me when I came home; but she coming first, they took her to the black hole [the town lock-up].

I waited for her return until I was tired, and then went to the house to know the reason; and having learned where she was, I immediately went down and gave myself up to one of the officers, named Thoburn. When I got into the watch-house, I told them who I was, and gave them to understand that I had sent her (Celia) away to go to London, and that I had not seen her since. In regard to their usage of me I shall not complain ; but I think that the way and manner in which Kennett was used by the keeper of the black hole ought to be made known.

He then launched into a bitter attack on the custodian of the lock-up, who ignored Kennett's pleas for a doctor when she was taken unwell soon after arriving there. This was despite the fact that she was pregnant and that the keeper was himself a family man. He finally brought her a little warm water in a basin, and told her that was more than she deserved – and this, fumed Holloway, was before any guilt was attributed to the woman. This outburst sums him and his hypocrisy up perfectly. For had he not a short time previously ended the life of his defenceless wife and her unborn child?

On Sunday, 14 August, the evening following that of their arrest, an inquest was held at the *Crown and Anchor* public house, Preston (which has survived and is located at 213 Preston Road). A bookcase was placed between Holloway and Kennett to prevent their communicating. The victim's sister, Catherine Bishop, testified as to Celia's troubled marriage, while a Dr Hargreaves told the coroner's jury that Celia had gone into labour when being murdered. Amelia Simmonds identified the pieces of wood which had been found as parts of Celia's trunk.

At the end a verdict of Wilful Murder was returned by the jury against Holloway and he was removed to Horsham Gaol. For her part, Ann Kennett was sent to Lewes House of Correction for further questioning.

The search was meanwhile on for the dismembered limbs and head of Celia Holloway. Daniel Manthorpe Folkard, Brighton's High Constable, and his officers targeted Margaret Street. Here they went through the lovers' rooms then decided to empty the common privy. Near the bottom, they made a dreadful discovery: the victim's arms still in their sleeves, her stockinged legs and, inside the mattress cover, her head.

Under questioning, Holloway continued to maintain that he had accompanied Celia to Preston whence she intended to catch a coach to London.

Ann, meanwhile, was asked to explain the shattered trunk. Since her answers were not satisfactory, she was remanded for a further

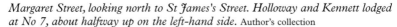

Margaret Street, looking north to St James's Street. Holloway and Kennett lodged at No 7, about halfway up on the left-hand side. Author's collection

Nos 7 and 8 Margaret Street in December 2003. The author

examination. This took place on 22 August at the *Sea House Hotel*, in Middle Street, Brighton (scheduled for demolition at the time of writing). She was further remanded for examination on Monday, 28 August, when her neighbours from Margaret Street spoke of seeing her and Holloway carrying a parcel late at night. She was remanded for a further week. At her final examination, it was acknowledged that she had not laid a finger on Celia in the fierce argument they had, but she had made repeated threats against her. The prisoner was bound over to appear at the Winter Assizes.

On Saturday, 27 August, Holloway, who had made more than one attempt to end his life, resolved to confess. He asked to see Edward Everard, the Brighton minister, who remembered

His cries, yes, almost his shrieks for the mercy of God upon his soul, were most humble, most appalling.

Holloway gave an account of all that had happened, unprompted, before three magistrates. He admitted that he had choked his wife and cut up her body. He gave the reason as her family's unkindness towards him. They had done all in their power to make him wretched and Celia herself had done all she could to destroy his peace of mind. He had therefore been driven to the act, for he had been bent on revenge.

In September, Holloway wrote a number of letters to his mother, and to his mother and sister jointly, which were permeated with religious fervour and repentance. He confessed his guilt yet was confident he would escape eternal damnation.

He next requested a meeting with Ann Kennett so that he could persuade her to reveal everything she knew. She was duly conveyed from Lewes to Horsham Gaol, but the encounter was a fraught one. Her first words, when they met in front of the magistrates, were, 'Oh, John, to what have you brought me?' Holloway energetically urged her to tell the full story. Turning on him, she violently hit the table and called him a 'deceptive wretch', 'villain', and 'blackguard'. He was, she exclaimed, possessed by the devil and trying to ruin her. His reply was that he could not be forgiven his crimes if he left this world without the full facts of the case being made known. But Kennett carried on abusing him, denying there was anything to tell. Her view was that he did not wish her to escape to marry someone else.

We might well wonder about Ann Kennett. A hammer, borrowed from a neighbour and never returned, had been found among some bloody rags found in the High Street lodgings. It had been washed and scraped clean – perhaps of blood. There had, after all, been a bruise on Celia's forehead. The hammer was not mentioned at Horsham Gaol.

Kennett and Holloway would not now meet until the trial and would never speak to each other again.

Holloway made three confessions and in the third curiously claimed that there were two Ann Kennetts. One – but not the one in custody – had aided him in the murder of Celia. She needed to be found and the Ann Kennett then held in Lewes released.

Holloway sent tender letters to Kennett from prison and even wrote to the High Constable of Brighton full of concern, repeating her request for her clothing. He also bequeathed her all his belongings. Yet nearer to the trial, he stated in a letter to the magistrates that he stood by his first two confessions. In so doing, he condemned Ann Kennett.

John Holloway was tried at Lewes Assizes on 15 December 1831 before Mr Justice Patteson. Ann Kennett was accused as an accessory of aiding and abetting him in the crime.

Dressed in his sailor's clothing, Holloway was in aggressive mood. On his way into court, a young boy pointed him out as someone he recognised. Holloway hit him hard in the face. When charged with murder, he claimed he did not understand a word of the indictment and insisted it be read a second time. His response, after a pause, was

By the laws of my country, my lord, I am not guilty; I am not guilty till you have proved me guilty. I am not guilty neither of several things stated there.

At every turn, he challenged witnesses in a hostile manner, refuting their statements. This was the man who, in prison, prayed and humbled himself before his Saviour and exhorted others to do the same. Now he was blaming Celia's family and the Overseers at Ardingly for his actions. He did at least tell the court that Ann Kennett was innocent. Any part she had played was, he said, because he had forced her.

During the proceedings, Kennett was tearful; she fainted and had to be physically supported; at one point she had to be taken out of the courtroom. Astonishingly, she was dismissed early in the proceedings. It was the judge's opinion that she was not guilty of murder, although new charges of being an accessory after the fact were to be brought against her.

At the end of the day-long trial, John Holloway was found guilty.

On Friday, 21 December, 1831, he was hanged at Horsham before a crowd of two thousand. While the executioner put on the cap and made fast the rope about the culprit's neck, Holloway said in a low whisper, 'Give me a good fall,' and the executioner therefore gave him rather more than the usual length of rope. The prisoner, who had taken the sacrament in the morning, then knelt down and prayed fervently for about half a minute, repeatedly calling on the Lord to receive his spirit. When he arose, he advanced suddenly to address the crowd, which he did in the following terms:

My dear friends, I need not tell you that sin brought me to this untimely end, and I would entreat you to be aware that he who follows a life of sin is as likely to be brought to the same condition; I tell you if you trifle with sin and folly, you know not where it will end. I justly suffer; I have spilt innocent blood, but I hope God will have mercy upon me; He has said to those who repent, 'All your sins and blasphemies shall be forgiven you.' Therefore, turn from sin, and the Lord will shew you forgiveness. All I have to say is take warning by my unhappy fate, and if you prize life sin not. Reflect on my dying words, for in a very short time the eye that sees you now will see you no more, and in a few short years you will all be in eternity. Now, may the Lord bless you and keep you from sin, by which I am brought to this untimely end; and may the God of Mercy, through Jesus Christ, receive my spirit.

These words were spoken rapidly, firmly and audibly and as he went on his voice rose to so high a tone that he could be heard at a great distance. He then stepped back. The executioner drew the cap over his eyes, while the chaplain continued to pray, concluding with the Lord's Prayer, during which Holloway, with great solemnity, repeatedly exclaimed, 'Lord, receive my spirit' until the signal was given for the bolt to be withdrawn. So his wretched life was ended. He appeared to suffer little. Among the crowd there was no manifestation of feeling nor any tokens of commiseration.

At this point, Nute took the stage. He mounted the wall on the left of the scaffold, and addressed the crowd, telling them that this was a most solemn time and exhorting them to flee from sin and take warning by the fate of Holloway. When he got down he told several persons standing in the garden that he had been with Holloway twelve hours previously, during which time he had, through the assistance of the Almighty, wrought such a change in him 'that he firmly believed the spirit of the culprit was now in bliss'. His hearers turned from him without deigning to reply.

After the body had hung a little while, a labourer from Cowfold with an unsightly wen on his forehead clambered up onto the staging. He asked if the lump could be touched by the corpse. Was not sweat from a dead man a sovereign cure? Holloway's wrists were untied and a handkerchief was placed on the still perspiring chest for the application. However, a similar request from two women was firmly refused by the hangman.

Holloway's corpse was sent back to Brighton by coach, in a trunk uncannily similar to that which had held Celia's torso. His body was put on display at the Town Hall for twenty-four hours and no fewer than 23,000 men, women and children came to view it. It was then removed to the hospital for dissection and for casts to be taken.

In March, Ann Kennett appeared at Lewes Assizes. She had a baby in her arms, which she had also named Ann. The charge against her was that of concealing and harbouring Holloway.

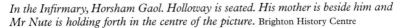

In the Infirmary, Horsham Gaol. Holloway is seated. His mother is beside him and Mr Nute is holding forth in the centre of the picture. Brighton History Centre

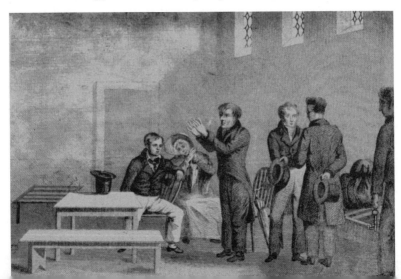

After brief proceedings, she was discharged. Her tearful plea of 'Not Guilty' won the sympathy of the judge and the jury were in turn swayed by his opinion. The content and tone of his address to the jury strike us today as astonishing, particularly the reference to the (absence of) guilt on the part of a wife:

The evidence against the prisoner is entirely circumstantial *and if you have any doubt, you must give the prisoner the benefit of that doubt. No wife can ever be found guilty of assisting her own husband, she might be guilty in some measure; but the law cannot touch her, and if the prisoner thought that she was the actual wife of Holloway, and you find such to have been her sincere belief, she must be acquitted of the crime as an accessory after the fact.*

Extraordinary.

His Lordship did, however, concede that Kennett seemed 'to have had some knowledge that Celia was his wife, from the circumstances which have arisen'. Kennett was nevertheless promptly acquitted.

In the case of John Holloway himself, justice was fully served. Society was spared any more devilry from his self-confessed 'savage nature'. With Celia's abominable murder, his prominent place in Brighton's hall of infamy is assured for ever.

★ ★ ★

When I visited the churchyard of St Peter's in Preston, Brighton, in October 2003 to see the plaque marking the last resting place of some of Celia Holloway's remains, there were two artificial red roses tied beneath it. Between them was the dried-out bud of a real rose.

Even now, somebody still cares.

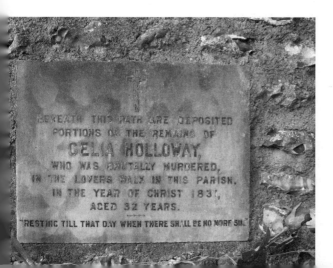

The plaque to Celia Holloway on the churchyard wall, St Peter's, Preston, Brighton. The author

CHAPTER 2

The Summer of 1934

I was never a violent man. Do I look like the sort of person who would kill a woman …?

(Toni Mancini, *Evening Argus*, 28.7.86)

To the north and east respectively of The Level recreation area, the eminent Brighton architect Amon Henry Wilds created the imposing terraces of Park Crescent and Hanover Crescent. The Level itself and Hanover Crescent date from 1822 but it was not until 1849, and then over a period of several years, that the residences forming Park Crescent came into being. The villas back onto a large private garden where once stood the county cricket ground, arguably the first in England, part of the long-vanished Royal Garden with its assembly rooms and other attractions. All forty-eight houses in the terrace are listed, save for Nos 24–26, which were erected in 1983 as facsimiles of houses bombed in 1942.

By the 1930s, the grand houses of Park Crescent had lost much of their elegance and many were divided into flats. To the then seedy basement property of No 44, in March 1934, came a young couple who gave their name as Watson. The man was purportedly a clothes-presser by trade. The occupation of his blonde, blue-eyed companion, seventeen years his senior, was not stated but involved personal service and would have dismayed Henry Snuggs, the landlord. He found them an affectionate couple and he was not to hear them quarrelling at any time.

In reality, Mrs Watson (she used the forename Joan) was a former music hall dancer named Violet Saunders, who preferred to be known as Violette Kaye. One of sixteen children, with a failed marriage behind her, she had turned to prostitution when work in shows became more difficult to obtain. To try and cope with the problems and setbacks in her life, she had taken to the bottle and, occasionally, morphine. Even though she was now 41, she was still attractive, so much so that many of her wealthier clients from the capital drove down to the coast to continue enjoying her services.

For his part, 'Mr Watson' was a thuggish small-time crook and former lightweight fairground boxer named Toni Mancini (other aliases were Luigi Mancini, Antoni Pirille, Hyman Gold and Jack Notyre). Swarthy in appearance and ruthless by temperament, he

A rear view of the houses in Park Crescent elegantly overlooking their garden.
Author's collection

Toni Mancini, the 'dancing waiter', a vicious thug turned murderer. Solo Syndication

Railings surround the basement of 44 Park Crescent where Violette Kaye met her end. The author

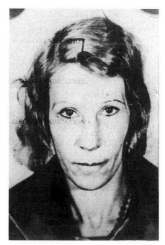

A soulful portrait of Violette Kaye, faded yet still attractive. Solo Syndication

had been born Cecil Lois England in 1908 in Newcastle upon Tyne. While still in his teens he had deserted from the RAF. He very soon became a member of London's underworld, working as a strong-arm man for a gangster named 'Harry Boy' Sabini. He admitted later 'I was a real tear-away and was actually getting kicks out of acts of violence.'

Displays of his ruthlessness on his 'rounds' included punishing an informer for life. Walking into the pub where the man was leaning on the bar, Mancini pulled an axe from under his coat, and chopped off his left hand. Coolly leaving the axe embedded in the bar, he walked out. Witnesses were afraid to talk and a cast-iron alibi was arranged for him by his associates. On another occasion, he punished a gangster who had dipped his hand into a till by turning the handle of a meat mincer while his victim's hand was forced into it. This story, however, he later dismissed as 'cobblers'.

Yet Mancini knew what it was like to suffer violence: when working as a bouncer at a night club, the injuries he received in a brawl were serious enough to put him in hospital for a time. Nor was he safe in Brighton: when strolling along the sea front one day with Violette, a young man sprang at him and slashed his face with a razor, then turned to attack her. Mancini managed to floor his assailant, who fled the scene.

It was in the previous September, just after Mancini had completed a six-month term for theft, that the couple had decided to move down from London to Brighton – 'the place to be' long before that catchphrase came into use.

The couple tended to move on average once a fortnight, doubtless when landlords found out why Violette had so many callers and because of problems due to her increasing alcoholism and addiction to morphine – and possibly also to evade people with a score to settle, like the promenade attacker. The basement flat at 44 Park Crescent, which the couple furnished using odds and ends bought at second-hand shops and markets, was their thirteenth home in the Brighton area – for Violette, the unluckiest of all. Previous addresses were lodgings in Devonshire Place, then Mighell Street, St George's Terrace, Clarendon Place, Russell Square, Stanley Road, Richmond Gardens, Hampton Place, Grand Parade, White Street, Edward Street, Lansdowne Place and Elm Grove.

To begin with, Mancini did the cooking and housework while Violette 'worked' in another part of the flat. When he talked of taking a job, she protested, as he would be away from her all day. He went ahead anyway, starting work on 5 May 1934 as a cook, waiter and general handyman at the Skylark Café, between the piers. He had, after all, been working in a restaurant near London's Alhambra Theatre, Leicester Square, when he and Violette met. Taking a job in Brighton got him out of the flat and gave him a chance to meet shady characters of his own kind – and plenty of young women.

Violette was aware of his interest in other females. Somewhat worse for drink, she turned up unexpectedly in the middle of the afternoon on Thursday, 10 May. It was not busy, so Mancini cooked her a meal then sat and talked to her while she ate. He then went off to get the staff their tea. A waitress, Florence Attrell, had started work at the café two days after Mancini and he handed the girl her tea, saying 'Here you are, mate'. Violette Kaye, her suspicions aroused, said in a loud voice, 'I won't have it. Don't call her mate.' The café went quiet and Mancini told her to pull herself together. An ugly scene was averted when she walked out. She sat outside for a time, then went away.

Mancini was to claim later that the quarrel cost him his job. This, however, was one of the inconsistencies in his recollections of that time. In fact, he turned up for work as usual the following morning, and told the other staff that Violette had left him and gone away to Paris. Violette's sister-in-law was due to come to

The basement front room at 44 Park Crescent, showing the cupboard in which Violette Kaye's body was placed, wrapped in bedclothes. Reproduced with the permission of the Chief Constable of Sussex, copyright reserved. ESRO Ref. SPA 11/3/4

Brighton for a holiday the following Monday. Instead she received a telegram: 'Good job sail Sunday will write – Vi.' It had not been sent by Violette. She was dead, killed by a number of blows to the head. Her body, wrapped in bedclothes, was lying in a cupboard in the Park Crescent basement flat.

That weekend, Mancini gave Florence Attrell some of Violette's clothes at the flat; he had, he said, promised to send them on but didn't think he would bother. He also took Florence out dancing twice.

It was time to find new lodgings. He told a sympathetic Mr Snuggs that Vi had walked out on him and that he could not afford to keep the flat on. To move the body, he had bought large strapped trunk in the market for 7s. 6d and had it delivered by the dealer. It was waiting in the middle of the room as they spoke. He left behind the tray out of the trunk, for which he had no use and, paying a man named Capelin to help him, pushed the trunk on a handcart to his new address. When he had gone, Snuggs noticed a stain in the bottom of the cupboard which someone had tried to wash away.

Mancini moved into lodgings at 52 Kemp Street, quite close to Brighton Station. For two months, he lived there with the increasingly odorous trunk containing the corpse of Violette Kaye. Fortunately for him, neither his landlord or landlady (Mr and Mrs Barnard) had any sense of smell. Outwardly unconcerned, Mancini must have been in turmoil by a discovery made just up the hill at the station's left luggage office on 17 June.

A locked trunk containing the torso of a young woman had been deposited there on Derby Day, June 6. It was opened 11 days later after railwayman William Vinnicombe became suspicious of the smell coming from it and called the police. The next day the legs were discovered in a suitcase at London's King's Cross station. The head and arms would never be found, although it was disclosed in March 1961, in an *Evening Argus* series 'Death in my Notebook' by Leonard Knowles, that the head had probably been found a week before the murder hunt without the police being aware of it.

It was on July 9 that the Yard and CID chiefs in charge of the inquiry into what was to be called 'Trunk Crime No 1' received a report which sent them racing to a small terraced house, 37 Blaker Street, off Edward Street. There they interviewed a young man, Mr Frederick Arthur Claridge, and his fiancée. They were told the following remarkable story, recounted in a report by Chief Inspector Robert Donaldson of the CID, New Scotland Yard:

Left: *52 Kemp Street, where Mancini lodged, with his trunk, for two months.* The author

Above: *The opening at Brighton Station of the first trunk.* Author's collection

... he disclosed that on the Sunday following Derby Day, viz. 10th June, he was with a friend, Miss Barbara Janet Maides, who resides at his address, and they were walking on the rocks under the cliff at Black Rock, at about 4 pm The tide at this time was out, and in one of the crevices containing a pool of water, they saw pieces of newspaper upon which were clots of blood. Their interest led them to inspect the pool further, and they saw what both declare to be a female human head. Miss Maides wanted to either pull the head out or to further satisfy her curiosity, but Mr Claridge compelled her to leave the spot as he thought some person had committed suicide by jumping from the cliff above and that the police, having taken away the remains they required, had swept the other portion into the sea.

It is difficult to speak with restraint as to why a normal and intelligent individual

William Vinnicombe, who discovered the torso in the trunk at Brighton Station, as caricatured in the Sunday Graphic. Author's collection

should form this view, but the fact remains that these two persons did observe what they described, for upon their arrival home they made mention of the matter to their landlady, and on the following morning, Claridge informed his employer. They all appeared to be satisfied with Claridge's reason for the presence in the pool of the blood and what appeared to be a head, and we became apprised of the knowledge through Claridge mentioning it to one of his employer's customers.

Inspector Pelling and I interviewed these two persons separately, and their stories were consistent, and indeed they were taken independently to the rocks under the cliffs where both pointed out spots, in near proximity, at which they had observed the details as shown.

Although it appeared futile, we gathered together our staff and searched the whole of this foreshore, and later invoked the aid of beachcombers, but having regard to the period that had elapsed, as anticipated, nothing was discovered.

It is possible that the head had been thrown into the sea from one of the piers and drifted eastwards.

Efforts were made by police on a mammoth scale to identify the victim in the trunk, who would in theory lead them to her killer. Over 800 women were reported missing and of these, 730 were traced. Examination of the contents revealed several layers of cheap common brown paper, under which was a parcel which almost completely filled the trunk; near the hinges a quantity of cotton wool had been packed and this was soaked with what appeared to be blood. The parcel was wrapped in brown paper of a similar description to the layers and the parcel was secured with thin sash cord, tied once lengthwise and three times across. The cord was cut and when a portion of the brown paper wrapping was pulled away, the contents were seen to consist of a human body from which the limbs and head had been removed.

The case and contents were conveyed to Brighton Police Station where Dr Pulling, the Brighton Police Surgeon, carried out an examination. He gave it as his opinion that the torso was the remains of a female possibly between the ages of 40 and 45, and that death had occurred during the preceding three weeks.

Every effort was made to establish who had been responsible for depositing the trunk at Brighton Station on Derby Day. It had borne a deposit counterfoil number CT.1945 but, in spite of exhaustive enquiries among the numerous staff, no progress was made. It was deduced from the ticket numbers that the trunk had been left some time during the afternoon of 6 June. The clerk on duty, Henry George Rout, thought it had been handed to him for deposit between the hours of 6 and 7 pm but, try as he might, he could not remember any detail of the person who had lodged the case.

At 6 pm on the day following the discovery in Brighton, the other trunk was opened by a cloakroom attendant at Kings Cross Railway Station for precisely the same reason that had prompted the attendant at Brighton Station to examine the one deposited there.

At the London terminus, it was found that the suitcase contained two human legs which had been severed at the knees. It was elicited that this case had been deposited on 7 June at about 1.30 pm and, as in the former discovery, no information whatever could be obtained as to the person responsible for its deposit. This case bore counterfoil number BE.8458.

Sir Bernard Spilsbury, the Home Office Pathologist, was requested to examine both trunk contents. His first examination was at Brighton Mortuary on Tuesday, 19 June 1934. In his subsequent report, he described the body as being that of a well-nourished woman, and stated that the amputations had been carried out using a sharp cutting instrument, the bones having been sawn across. He made the interesting discovery that the woman had been between four and five months pregnant and that the pregnancy had not in any way been interfered with. He thought it unlikely that the victim had previously given birth to a full-term child. There were no scars on the torso and no natural disease could be found to account for death, neither was there indication of poisoning or marks of violence. He added that dismemberment had taken place several hours, at least, after death by a person not skilled in anatomical knowledge.

Spilsbury remarked on the unusual feature of the complete absence of blood in the trunk, which led him to conclude that the dismemberment had been carried out some time before the torso had been placed in it. He estimated the age of the victim to be around 25 years, in contrast to Pulling, and her height 5' 3" to 3½". The colour of the hair was given as light brown.

He next examined the limbs at Paddington Mortuary and subsequently reported that they were part of the human remains belonging to the torso and that they bore no scars. He described the victim's feet as regular and well-formed, 9 inches in length; the toenails were clean and well cared-for. This suggested that the woman wore well-fitting shoes and, coupled with the fact that the armpits of the torso had recently been shaved, that she was particular in matters of personal hygiene.

In the Kings Cross trunk, a quantity of brown paper wrappings had been used to cover the limbs, which had been secured by a length of string. This paper was found to be saturated with what appeared to be oil, and in addition there were found in this case two issues of the *Daily Mail*, dated 21 May and 2 June 1934.

Neither trunk yielded fingerprints, although when the brown paper was examined at Brighton Police Station on 17 June, a piece was found which bore in blue pencil the letters, 'FORD'. The first part of the word had been destroyed by the blood which had oozed from the torso.

It was assumed the perpetrator of this crime would also use a left luggage office or offices to dispose of the head and arms. Special insertions were therefore placed in the *Police Gazette* on 19 and 20 June 1934, detailing the discoveries and requesting that enquiries be made at all cloakrooms and other likely places. In the Metropolitan Police Area, the position was dealt with by an 'All Stations' message requesting immediate enquiries to be made at every railway station cloakroom and other likely place. To spread the net still wider, Brighton's Chief Constable sent a communication to the Chief of Police of each of the four national groups of railway companies asking for their cooperation and assistance. The maximum use was made of police publications and the press to circulate the details of the victim as supplied by Sir Bernard Spilsbury in a bid to home in on the killer.

The trunks themselves were found to be new and of the cheaper kind, the one left at Brighton having been made that year by Sewells of Shepherds Bush while the suitcase deposited at Kings Cross had been manufactured by Messrs Lewis and Co of Leyton. As for the brown paper, intensive examination led to the discovery that some portion of it, when pieced together, formed what appeared to be a large brown paper bag. Sheets of brown paper in the Kings Cross case which appeared to be saturated in oil were submitted for analysis. The oil turned out to be a vegetable oil, such as might be used for cooking or household purposes, and such a quantity was obtained from one sheet that it was clear that considerable use had been made of it. A small hair or fibre was found after a microscopic test, this being discovered in the corner of the portion of the brown paper bag taken for analysis. This item was found to have come from either from the plane tree or the mullein plant. A putty or fawn-coloured trouser button, adhering to which was a portion of sewing thread or cotton, was found in the Kings Cross case, but this did not prove to be of any assistance. Nor did the cotton wool found in the trunk at Brighton, which consisted of a cheap variety of wool such as might be used for packing and not of the type used in surgical cases. It could be purchased at almost any stores retailing cheap or common household articles, as could a face flannel also found in the Brighton trunk.

So the investigation made little progress, save in the matter of the part-word 'FORD', found on a piece of brown paper contained in the Brighton trunk. The police were able to secure a definite assertion by a person that she was responsible for writing the letters. This came about following a visit to New Scotland Yard on 30 July 1934, by Miss Ethel Moysey, of Cricklewood, who was employed as secretary to the Loraine Confectionery Company, Station Road, Finsbury Park. This company had eleven shops in the metropolis and five at Eastbourne, and the main stock in these shops was supplied by Meltis Limited of Bedford, the parent company. When goods were forwarded by Meltis to Finsbury Park it became the duty of a Mr Maurice Linder, the Manager of the Loraine Confectionery Company, to inspect the deliveries and, if defects were discovered, Miss Moysey and other assistants repacked the goods to be returned. After the articles were ready, Miss Moysey wrote upon the parcel in blue pencil the words 'Meltis, Bedford', and the goods were subsequently collected for conveyance.

There appeared to be no question whatsoever that Miss Moysey was indeed responsible for writing the letters 'FORD', so enquiries were made as to what happened to the brown paper wrappings when they arrived at Bedford. She produced sheets of brown paper identical in texture to those used at the Finsbury Park Depot. These were cut in half when received and this was found to be the case in the Brighton trunk, where the paper was cut in an identical manner to those used by Miss Moysey.

When visiting the Bedford factory, Chief Inspector Sharpe learned that the sheets of brown paper received in circumstances as described by Miss Moysey were used in repacking goods which were despatched to various parts of the country, including a depot at Brighton. He actually inspected the whole of the Meltis works, and the position of the staff employed there was reviewed. It emerged that the only reason Miss Moysey had visited New Scotland Yard was because she felt that Mr Linder of the Finsbury Park Depot was connected with this crime. He was a married man, reputed to be on familiar terms with several girls, and since early in June he had appeared very worried and distressed. As he was away on holiday, Miss Moysey had thought it a good time to convey her suspicions to the police. A close watch was kept on his movements and on his return, he and an associate named George Joslin were interviewed but they were able to prove that they could not have been responsible for the deposit of the cases at Kings Cross or Brighton.

The only avenue remaining to the police was a careful examination of reports of missing females. Some came in from friends who had not seen Violette Kaye for a while. There was also gossip about her affair with Toni Mancini. When this spread, Knowles went to see him, asking searching questions. 'Did she keep him?' he asked the rather shabby-looking waiter:

> *Yes, I suppose you could put it like that … Where might she be? I really don't know, but it wouldn't surprise me if she'd gone abroad.*

All the time, of course, he was sleeping only a few feet away from her decomposing body.

After a month of investigation, Donaldson of the Yard and Brighton's Detective Inspector Arthur Pelling also homed in on Mancini. On 14 July 1934, the suspect went willingly to the police station under the Town Hall and made a detailed statement. Donaldson was to report:

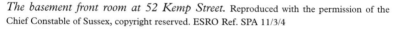

The basement front room at 52 Kemp Street. Reproduced with the permission of the Chief Constable of Sussex, copyright reserved. ESRO Ref. SPA 11/3/4

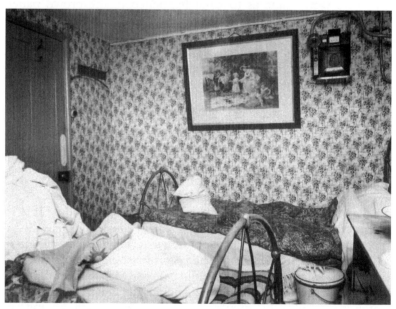

Sergeant Sorrell and Chief Inspector Pelling of Brighton CID discussing the case with pipe-smoking Chief Inspector Robert Donaldson of Scotland Yard. Solo Syndication

He gave the name of Cecil Lois England, aged 26 years, and went on to refer to his association with the woman 'Violette Kaye' with whom he had lived as man and wife at various addresses in Brighton. He denied knowing that the woman was a prostitute which was palpably untrue, and concluded by asserting that upon arriving home one evening, he found a note from Kaye in which she expressed her intention of leaving him to go with a man who was able to keep her. He gave the date of this occurrence as the 14th May, 1934, and suggested that as the woman had been very friendly with a Commission Agent named Cooper, it was more than probable that she had decamped with him. He told his story with perfect composure and was able to conclusively prove that he was at work on the material dates affecting the deposit of the cases at Brighton and Kings Cross and that it would have been impossible for him to have taken part in either of these acts.

We had been told that he had given away certain articles of feminine attire, but he denied this and in view of the fact that he had definitely cleared his position with regard to the crime we were interested in, coupled with the knowledge that Violette Kaye bore no resemblance whatever to the victim of the crime, Mancini was released. He returned to his place of employment after the interview, and carried out his usual duties without betraying any unusual signs and indeed we learned that later in the evening, he visited and danced at a local Dance Hall.

Ironically, the trunk murder team had already made a routine check at 52 Kemp Street, but the owners of the boarding house had been away and no police search had been made of the rooms. The pressure was now, however, well and truly on Mancini, who was in a state of near panic:

> *I just didn't know what to do with Violette's body. You can imagine my dilemma. When the police started checking along Kemp Street, I just got all my money together – £4 – and took the first train to London.*

He left not a moment too soon.

The police had been alerted by a painter and decorator working at the house to obnoxious smells emanating from the basement in Kemp Street, and Chief Inspector Donaldson directed Sergeants Sorrell and Scales of the Brighton Force to visit that address on 15 July 1934 and carry out an inspection.

The inevitable gruesome discovery was made and on the same day Sir Bernard Spilsbury conducted a post-mortem examination

Violette Kaye's body, found under a bloodstained overcoat, in the trunk taken from Kemp Street. Reproduced with the permission of the Chief Constable of Sussex, copyright reserved. ESRO Ref. SPA 11/3/4

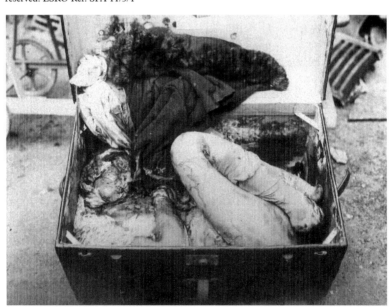

which revealed that Violette Kaye had died as the result of a fractured skull due to a severe blow on the side of the head with some heavy instrument.

Donaldson – who identified a photograph of Jack Noytre as that of 'Mancini' – recorded:

> *... it was found that although he had gone to 52 Kemp Street, at 12.30 am, on the 15th July, he had not in fact slept there. Apparently he sensed that we intended to make further enquiry, for after leaving a Local Dance Hall, he met two young men and requested them to accompany him to Kemp Street at the time shown, and after packing a few articles, he and the two men left the house at 3 am. Mancini indicated his intention of proceeding to London, and the three men walked about until 7 am, when Mancini joined a train at Preston Park Station en-route for London.*

He was not to remain at large for long – 48 hours in fact. A massive hue and cry was raised and details of the latest discovery were now in all the newspapers.

When in London, the suspect could find no refuge among his gangland associates. He spent his brief remaining period of freedom eating in cheap East End cafés and sleeping in a Salvation Army hostel. At one point he picked up a 17-year-old waif, Doris Saville. He took her for a walk and asked her to provide him with an alibi for the murder. This was that they had visited Violette at Park Crescent for tea on May 10, they had left her alone with three men while going for a walk, and on returning had found her dead. She agreed, but only because she was in fear of him. She would later testify against him at the Assizes.

Finally, Mancini decided to quit the metropolis and set out for Kent. At 1.35 am on 17 July 1934, PCs Gourd and Triplow, whilst patrolling in a car, observed a man walking towards Sidcup. He appeared 'nervous and hesitant' and they therefore stopped him. He subsequently admitted his identity ('I'm the man. But I didn't murder her . . .') and was accordingly conveyed to Lee Road Police Station.

Donaldson later attended there with Detective Inspector Pelling and Sergeant Sorrell. After the customary caution, Mancini volunteered a statement in which he sought to show that he was not responsible for Violette Kaye's death. He alleged he had returned home one evening from work at the 'Skylark' on about 14 May 1934 and found her on the bed, dead, with a handkerchief around her neck. There was blood everywhere. He had not had the courage to inform police as he feared he might be blamed and would not be able to prove his innocence.

He had then obtained a black trunk and placed the body in this, and inferred that a man named Kay Fredericks, with whom the victim had at one time cohabited, might be responsible for her death. Fredericks was, of course, quickly eliminated from the enquiry. Mancini was charged under the name of Jack Notyre with wilful murder and taken back down to Brighton to face the accusation.

Leonard Knowles was among the throng awaiting the prisoner's return:

> *There were several entrances to the building, but the actions of a mounted policeman gave me a real indication of the door which was to be used. He rode his horse on to the pavement and then cleared people from the steps leading to the main door of the building, and I at once stationed myself inside, taking the risk that some other door would be chosen and I would miss seeing the arrival. But I was lucky. Three minutes later a car drove at speed up to the building and stopped with a jerk close to the four stone steps leading up to the door. In the back seat were Inspector Pelling and Sergeant Sorrell with Mancini between them. He was handcuffed to the sergeant's left wrist. Anxious not to lose a second in getting Mancini into the building before the crowd surged across the road, Inspector Pelling jumped out and pulled hard on Mancini's left arm to drag him out of the car.*
>
> *There was a sharp exclamation of pain from Sergeant Sorrell, and Mancini's face broke into a smile. The prisoner was out of the car and into the building a split second before a huge crowd ran towards the main doors, which were slammed shut and secured. Mancini looked straight at me standing there, and evidently recognised me from having interviewed him. He gave me a fleeting smile.*
>
> *'Not guilty,' he whispered as he was hurried past and down a flight of stairs to the cells. He looked very tired and extremely pale.*

Mancini's hearing was set for 10 December 1934 and he spent much of the intervening period in Brixton Prison. The trial, before Mr Justice Branson, was a grand affair, with public admission by ticket only (applications had been received from far and wide, one coming from France and another from Belgium). J D Cassels KC, MP (Recorder for Brighton) and the Hon. Quintin Hogg were Counsel for the prosecution, while Mancini was defended by Norman Birkett KC, John Flowers KC and Eric Neve.

A powerful case had been built up against the prisoner. There was the evidence of his bloodstained clothing (human blood was found on three of his shirts and two pairs of his trousers), the hammer recovered from the basement, his admission of forging the telegram to Violette's sister, and the numerous witness depositions testifying to his aggressiveness towards Violette Kaye and total lack of concern as to her disappearance and whereabouts. Possession of the trunk and fleeing from Brighton would surely seal his fate.

Doris Saville and Skylark waitress Joyce Golding added their powerful testimony against Mancini. He told Golding, a prostitute, that Violette had gone to Montmartre on a two years' contract and that he was glad she had gone, adding: 'Now she won't follow me about the streets nagging and calling me names.' He had asked Golding to live with him, but she had declined. Florence Attrell confirmed his shirt was bloodstained and that she washed it. She was told Violette had run away to Paris with her uncle.

Birkett turned the trial on its head. His brilliance as an advocate was revealed in these proceedings more than perhaps in any other. Stone by stone he demolished the prosecution case, yet he had little to go on save the one basic fact in favour of the accused: no one could prove that it was his hand that had killed Violette Kaye.

Golding's evidence was, he said, in distinct contrast to that of other witnesses who had been closer to Violette. Saville for her part had, he pointed out, given very different evidence earlier at the magistrates court. Then she had said that Mancini had told her that he was innocent of murder and that he wanted her help, not to cover up murder but to avoid being wrongly accused.

The murder weapon, Birkett argued, would surely not have been left on the premises but dropped from the end of the pier. Violette was a prostitute and the killer could have been one of her customers. It was claimed that the afternoon Mancini and Kaye had quarrelled, a man named Kerslake had called at their flat to tell Violette that one of her regular clients had just been certified insane. She had come to the door looking upset and shaken, and seemed to be drunk. Kerslake could hear voices in the back room. So Violette had had visitors after her quarrel with Mancini and one of these could have been her killer.

Pathologist Sir Bernard Spilsbury was made to concede that the injury to the dead woman's forehead could have been caused by a fall down the narrow and worn basement steps. A police inspector had been made to testify as to their state. Another

The basement area and steps, 44 Park Crescent. The author

pathologist, Dr Roche Lynch, was made to admit that he was not sure whether Violette Kaye had died from morphine. Birkett even took the extraordinary step of insisting that Mancini's previous convictions – two for stealing and one for loitering with intent – be read in court. He wanted to establish that his client had never been convicted for violence (the hatchet and meat grinder episodes were, understandably, kept under wraps).

He called a tailor, Walter Robert Blaker, of Kemp Street, who told the court that, although Mancini had ordered the suit to which one pair of trousers belonged during May, he had not received it until June. He was not in possession of the trousers at the time Violette died. This remarkable revelation began to raise real doubts in the minds of the jury.

When the prisoner was called, he made a favourable impression on the jury; he disarmingly told Birkett that he had loved Violette and went as far as to declare that they had never quarrelled. He took a rosary from his pocket and at one point even shed a few tears. When asked why he had not fetched the police when he found Violette's body he asked incredulously, 'With my record?'.

The thrust of the brilliant defence submission was that the prosecution had not proved Mancini had killed Violette Kaye. In his closing speech, Birkett made the shrewd point that the 'voices' Kerslake had heard in Violette Kaye's flat on the day of her murder had never come forward. Then there was the question of motive:

Why did he do it? There hasn't been a word. There has been no word, no question, no hint, no suggestion of any kind, as to that vital matter as to why he should do it, and upon that vital question, the answer is complete and impenetrable silence.

On 14 December 1934, after one of the finest defences ever heard in a British court of law, the jury, which had been out for nearly two and a half hours, brought in their verdict. The *Sussex Daily News* reported:

Prisoner still remained below while the jury answered to their names. Then the Judge came into the Court, and prisoner, wearing an overcoat he had not previously worn, resumed his place in the dock.

The Clerk of Assize put to the jury the question: Gentlemen of the jury, are you agreed upon your verdict ?

'We are,' replied the Foreman.

'How say you,' asked the Clerk, 'do you find the prisoner guilty or not guilty?'

'NOT GUILTY,' responded the Foreman.

The words re-echoed around the Court, and the prisoner appeared to be almost in a state of collapse as he realized their meaning. Meanwhile his father sat with bowed head, and it was some moments before he appeared to be conscious of what had happened.

The Judge's only comment was: 'You are discharged,' and Mancini, a free man, staggered down the steps of the dock to be released after having been a prisoner since 18th July.

This was a personal triumph for Norman Birkett, to whom Mr Cassels himself had earlier paid tribute by remarking:

the prisoner had the services of one who held, and rightly and deservedly held, the reputation for being one of the most skilful advocates at the Bar. No defence in any Court could have been more skilfully conducted.

The police were furious about the verdict. Not only had Trunk Crime No 1 defeated them (it would never be solved) but the vast operation of bringing Mancini to what they believed to be justice had come to nought.

For a year after his trial, Mancini worked in a travelling fair. Billed as 'Toni Mancini, the Infamous Brighton Trunk Murder Man', he used a mock guillotine with which he pretended to chop off the head of a pretty girl. Later years were spent roaming the world and there were two broken marriages, although he found happiness in a third – and a new life in the north of England.

Over forty years after the trial, at the age of 69, he was persuaded to give an interview at his home to *News of the World* reporter Alan Hart. The issue for 28 November 1976 contained a startling confession and appeared with the headline I'VE GOT AWAY WITH MURDER. In it, Mancini gave the following vivid account of what happened to Violette Kaye on that fateful day in May after she had visited the 'Skylark':

> *She was legless drunk and doped up to the eyeballs. I called a taxi and got her home about 4 pm By this time she was starting to suffer from withdrawal symptoms.*
>
> *It was a lovely summer's day, but she was shivering and asked me to make a fire for her. Our argument was still going on, and while she lay on the bed I went to the cellar to bring back some coal and the hammer for breaking it into small pieces.*
>
> *I broke the coal up and put the hammer down. I had just lit the paper and was blowing it to get the fire started when I felt a crack on the head. It was Violette, and she was hitting me with the hammer. I managed to get it off her and started to walk towards the cellar with it.*
>
> *She shouted to me 'Give me that hammer.' I said: 'I'll give you the hammer all right.' Then I threw it across the room at her with all my strength. It caught her on the left temple and she spun round twice like something on a fairground. Her eyes were bulging out of her head. Then she fell like a ton of bricks on the brass fireplace surround. I ran over to her and shouted: 'You stupid bitch. Look what you've made me do.'*
>
> *As I was shouting, I was holding her by the shoulders and banging her head up and down. I thought I was banging it on the floor, but I later discovered I was banging her head on the fireplace surround. Suddenly blood started to trickle from her mouth and I froze. I realised what I'd done.*
>
> *I honestly didn't mean to kill her – I had just lost control of myself in the heat of the moment. The whole thing had happened in less than a minute. I felt for a heartbeat and there was none. She had no pulse. I took a make-up mirror from her handbag and held it against her mouth. Nothing.*
>
> *I thought: 'This is it. You've just gone and got yourself hanged.' I didn't know what to do. I was in a real state. The rest of the story after that is the version I gave at the trial.*

As for the trial itself, he confessed:

When I gave evidence I had carefully rehearsed my lines like an actor. I had practised how I should hold my hands and when I should let the tears run down my cheeks.

It might sound cold and calculating now, but you have to remember that my life was at stake. I was charged with murder and in those days the penalty was death. It's remarkable how convincing you can make lies sound when you're fighting for your life. I never really expected to be acquitted, but I always held on to the faint hope.

None of the public, except my parents and the odd friend who stayed loyal, wanted me to get off. Hundreds of people turned up like ghouls to boo and hiss at me every time I appeared in court. They were shouting for my blood outside the assizes after the 'not guilty' verdict, and I had to leave by a rear exit to avoid being lynched.

The judge had his black hat all ready to sentence me to death. Then the jury foreman announced the decision. I'll never forget the look on that judge's face when he said: 'You are discharged.' I felt that if looks could kill, I would have been executed on the spot.

Two years after his confession, Mancini gave an interview to journalist Stephen Knight (shortly before the latter's death). In that, he gave a considerably different account of the quarrel and what led up to it. He said he had been working in the Skylark Café 'about three or four months' and Violette had no idea of where to find him. One day she came into the café very drunk and under the influence of drugs, and caused a scene. He picked her up by the shoulders and carried her outside, and she finally went home. When he got home at about 7 o'clock that evening, there was a violent quarrel and 'she came at me with her hands and scratched my face.' Then she picked up the hammer and tried to hit him with it. 'So I hit her.' Violette fell against the brass fender, and when he tried to pick her up, she spat in his face. Mancini insisted, 'I'd never hit her before ... I don't hit women.' But on this occasion:

I just got hold of her, of her shoulders, and was banging her head on the floor like that. I said, 'Don't you spit at me!' And I don't know how long I was like that. And when I came to out of my rage, she was lying like that... quite still you see.

Knight asked:

'So what killed her was not the accidental fall... it was you banging her head on the fender?'
'Yes ...I don't remember really, but that's what I must have done ...'

As a result of these revelations, a senior Sussex detective was given the task of reopening the infamous Brighton trunk murders file. However, the Director of Public Prosecutions stated that independent corroboration of Mancini's claim was essential and because of the years elapsed between 1934 and 1976 this would not now be available. In a letter to the Chief Constable of Sussex he officially closed the Mancini case by stating that in his opinion there was insufficient evidence available, or likely to become available, to prosecute Mancini for perjury.

Interestingly, the Sussex police were contacted after the 1976 revelations by a W C Clifford, aged 66, from Gloucester, who said he had served with Mancini in the RAF in 1940 in the Gloucestershire Transport Department. He remembered Mancini using the name Tony England and recalled him bragging quite openly of having done the murder and disposing of the body. A Mr Jack Williams, aged 64, from Portslade, also similarly remembered Mancini bragging he had killed a woman and believed it was almost immediately after he was acquitted.

The man who actually did get away with murder had left Alan Hart, and readers across the country, with the following thoughts:

Of course I feel ashamed and guilty about what happened. But although I had told lies to get off that murder charge, there were mitigating circumstances which might have won me some sympathy. Under today's laws, I would probably have got away with manslaughter but not then. The truth is that I didn't really mean to kill her. In those days, it would have been impossible to tell the truth and escape the gallows. So I did what any man would do. I did everything I could to save my life.

I'm married to a wonderful woman, living a normal happy life. Apart from you, she's the only person who knows the full story about me. And she thinks so much of me that she refuses to believe I could do such things.

I'm not proud of the things I've done – quite the opposite. But when you've harboured a guilty secret like mine all these years, it's a great relief to tell somebody. People will still think I've been a real villain and maybe they won't forgive me. But at least I hope they will understand.

At the end of July 1986, in a further twist, *Evening Argus* reporter Carolyn Robertson tracked Mancini down to an address in South London, where he was living under an assumed name. In the interview, the frail 78-year-old protested his innocence in respect of both trunk killings and vowed to fight the 'lies' until the day he died. Sitting in an armchair in the living room of the flat he shared with his wife, Peggy, Mancini vowed:

I'll go to the end of the earth and bring the whole of them down with
me if they try to connect me with that murder.

He was referring to Trunk Crime No 1 but in the same conversation
hotly reneged on the confession made to the *News of the World*.

Curiously, the police had reopened their investigations on the
basis of testimony from an old gardener from Wiltshire. Herbert
Porter, 71, of Sutton Benger had only then come forward to say
he recognised Mancini as the man who asked him to help
transport a trunk to Great Summerford railway station for
loading on a train to Waterloo. The '-ford' of 'Summerford' was
allegedly the part-word found on the bloodstained luggage label.
Detective Chief Superintendent Drummond Marvin actually
believed he might still be able to find the victim's skull. This was
in response to a theory that the mystery woman's killer or killers
may have thrown her skull onto a bonfire (a charred skull was
found on a riverbank where a bonfire had been burning at the
time and was handed to a museum curator). Marvin stated:

> *The inquiry is not being closed. We still have a lot of work to do …*
> *We believe the skull could have been discarded near Great*
> *Summerford and so inquiries will centre it down there. If we find the*
> *skull we could still ask to re-examine the contents of the victim's*
> *grave* [in Brighton] *to see if we can match the remains.*

Mancini denied ever having been to Wiltshire. He wondered why
a 50-year-old case was being brought up again. As for Violette
Kaye, reports of his killing her were 'totally untrue and blown up
out of all proportion.' He declared:

> *What I said then was true. I was on oath and a jury of 12 people*
> *cleared me. I don't know who killed her but someone else did.*

Mancini and his wife were now a well-respected couple and none
of their friends knew about his past. Peggy, equally frail, defended
her husband, who had had a stroke a year earlier:

> *He's a very sick man and it's not fair on a man at his age to drag*
> *this up after all these years. He's had X-rays but the doctors wouldn't*
> *say what they found. He says only got six months to live, so please*
> *leave us alone.*

It is tempting to think that Mancini's conscience was clear. The
trouble is, he never had one.

JOURNEY'S END

CHAPTER 3

The Lonely Death of George Griffith
1849

He examined the body, took hold of it, tried to move it and said, 'Get up' or something of that sort but still received no answer.

The Rock Brewery in Brighton was established at 61 St James's Street in about 1809 and stood at the corner of Mount Street, with premises also in Warwick Street and St Mary's Place. It continued brewing until 1928, when it was amalgamated with Portsmouth and United Breweries Ltd. 'Rock Ale' was well-known throughout the town and, indeed, across the county, but today nothing remains of the brewery or malthouses.

In 1846-52, the company was listed in a local directory as Griffith & Co. Its principal proprietor was George Stonhouse

The Rock Brewery as seen from the seaward end of Atlingworth Street. Chris Horlock collection

Montpelier Crescent and environs from the air. The Argus

Griffith, aged 42, who had moved to Brighton in November 1845 to join Isaac Sewell, Manager of the Branch County Bank at Brighton, as partner in the business. Since his arrival, he had built up a wide circle of friends and won the respect of many, both within and outside his employment. He was an active member of the town's Commissioners and a highly intelligent man. His home life, too, was all that could be desired, and he lived with his wife and two fine sons, one aged eight and the other ten, in a substantial residence, 25 Montpelier Crescent. Luckily for them, Griffith had insured his life only ten days before he met his end.

His chief clerk was William Shubrick Martin, who on 11 January 1849 received a strange anonymous letter, postmarked Trafalgar Street. It was written in a disguised hand, although evidently by a person who had had a tolerable education.

It read (with spelling errors) as follows:

Mr Martins, Grffith's brewery, Brighton.
SIR, – Some parties intend to rob you next time you goes to Horsham, so bee on your gard.

Martin later stated:

.. he had some business at Horsham, and he wished to go. Two pistols were taken by Mr Griffith, with two powder flasks and some bullets

Like Park Crescent, Montpelier Crescent near the Seven Dials was the creation of Amon H Wilds. It was erected in 1843–7 on a site which had been a cricket ground known as Lillywhite's, Lee's Trap or the Temple Fields Ground. Engraving by Newman & Co., published by W Grant of Castle Square, Brighton. Mike Felmore collection

from his counting house on Monday, for the purpose of taking with him on this journey the following morning. They are not his property, but were borrowed by me of Mr Wallace, excise-officer, in consequence of having received the above note, and thinking I should have to go to Horsham. Mr Griffith also took a six-barrel revolving pistol, but this he did not take with him. … It was my intention to have accompanied Mr Griffith on this journey; but, on speaking to him on Monday, he said he had a friend staying with him whom he wished to take for a ride, and that he did not see any necessity for both to go, unless I did.

At that time, larger firms did not use commercial travellers for visits to their customers. The custom was for the journey to be made by the head of the company or one of his sons. In this way a personal rapport was established and fostered between the business and its clients.

In the case of his own company, Griffith had followed this practice of visiting public houses out in the country, collecting accounts due and taking orders for the renowned 'Rock Ales.' For some months, however, it had been Martin who had been performing this duty. The day set aside for these visits was the first Tuesday in every month.

February 6 was therefore the appointed day for Griffith's journey. Late in the evening, he was back in Horsham, having

Griffith's villa today, secluded by trees and shrubs. The author

passed through in the morning and made a number of calls during the day. Yet a Mr Gumbrell, a Poynings brewer, later told how there had been two strange men in the village on that Tuesday, making inquiries as to the relative distances between Newtimber, Poynings, and other places. Griffith was at the *Horse and Groom* at Horsham, a house which he served, when the landlady, Mrs Maria Ansell, remarked on several robberies having taken place in the West Grinstead area. He said he was not afraid. He had never hurt anyone, and he thought no one would

Dale Gate in the early 1900s. The road from Henfield is on the left. Author's collection

hurt him; he then took a red bag from the right hand pocket of his greatcoat, out of which he drew a pistol, and having unscrewed the barrel, he loaded the weapon. Having put this in his pocket, he took out another pistol, but said he would not load that at present. He remarked 'The other will be enough for one man. You needn't fear that I shall give up my money easily.'

Taking his leave of Mrs Ansell, he climbed into his gig and drove to Henfield, where he had one last business call to make. This was at the *White Hart*. He arrived at about 8.30 and sat down to a meal with the landlady of the inn, collected an account due from her, and stopped a few minutes longer to play with her children. Just before nine he had his horse and gig brought to the door and set out briskly on the last stage home.

It was a damp and hazy evening yet, despite the moon being frequently obscured, very light. On the road between Henfield and Brighton were two turnpikes, one called Terry's Cross Gate and, some three miles further south, one named Dale Gate. At five past nine, Griffith reached Terry's Cross Gate in Woodmancote parish but did not stop, having paid his toll in the morning.

Between the two turnpikes, the road was lonely, rough and steep, sloping up to the Downs on one side. Griffith had to walk his horse up the hill towards Newtimber Church, and again up the following ascent, which was just a quarter of a mile short of Dale Gate in Pyecombe parish. The keeper's wife was one Harriet Crosskey:

At about half-past nine last night, I was standing outside of my house, on the west side. I was looking for Mr Griffith, whom we had been expecting for some time, and whilst there I heard a 'shriek hello' – only once. It appeared to come from the west road, and appeared to me as if it came from some person in pain. The wind was in the south-west and was very low. I did not hear the noise of wheels. I was waiting for Mr Griffith, who usually returned by half-past eight or nine at latest, and I listened after that for some time but heard nothing. Nothing passed the gate afterwards that night.

Sounds of distress were also heard by Richard Pelling Jnr, a labourer living at Newtimber with his father about a quarter of a mile to the north-east of the spot where Mr Griffith would be found, on the west road:

Whilst I was going to bed at about twenty minutes past ten last night I heard the sound as of a man groaning – three or four groans. They seemed to me to come up from the west road, and were very loud. I spoke about it to my father … He opened the window, and we heard the groans again two or three times. They were hardly half-a-minute apart. We did not go out to see what the groans were and did not hear any body pass down the road. I mentioned what I had heard at 5 o'clock this morning to my master, Mr Mannington.

Another employee of William Mannington was one George Tidey, who at around 9.30 pm, heard 'the report of fire-arms' from the stable door where he was standing. It appeared to come from the west. 'My master's stable', he deposed, 'is not quite a quarter of a mile from the spot where the body was found.' Sarah Ann Smoker, a schoolmistress of Newtimber, said she heard one report of a gun or pistol, apparently coming from the direction of Mr Mannington's buildings, but thought no more of it.

The lifeless Griffith was discovered at about 2 o'clock in the morning. Two brothers from Hove, Charles and James Hodson, and their companion Charles Kirton, had been dining at the residence of a Mr Laurence Smith in Woodmancote. This was Terry's Lodge, a house standing in its own grounds close to the road about a mile from Henfield. They were returning home in a light cart. James Hodson saw a man lying on the roadside, his head resting on the bank and as he approached him, saw a hat lying beyond him. He stopped, telling his brother to get down and investigate. Charles got down and spoke to the person, but received no answer. He examined the body, took hold of it, tried to move it and said, 'Get up' or something of that sort but still received no answer. Charles Kirton then alighted and he immediately recognised the body. 'Why, it is Griffith!' he exclaimed, and putting his hand on his face, found it cold and immediately added, 'He is dead.'

James Hodson then picked up a pistol by the side of the body and a pair of spectacles covered with black crepe, which had obviously been used as a mask. A little further off they found a whip. They put the body into the cart to take to the *Plough* public house at Pyecombe. There they observed the single pistol shot wound in the chest which had ended the unfortunate brewer's life. They lost no time in informing the nearest constable and made their way to Brighton with all possible speed.

Clearly the victim had fought for his life. A button found wrenched from its fastening showed his great-coat had been torn open and there were mudstains on his clothes in places. There was also evidence that he had taken off a glove to reach for one of the pistols in his pocket. In the heat of the moment, however, he had unfortunately drawn out the wrong weapon, since the loaded pistol was found in his coat pocket. A subsequent police examination indicated that an attempt had been made to use the unloaded firearm.

The now broken driving-whip had doubtless been used in self-defence. The harness reins had been cut, evidently with a clasp knife found nearby. Searchers also discovered the hat, an empty 'steel bead' purse and the spectacles. The assailant's

The key locations in the Griffith case. A Brighton woman was murdered in Shaves Wood in 1939. Susan Rowland

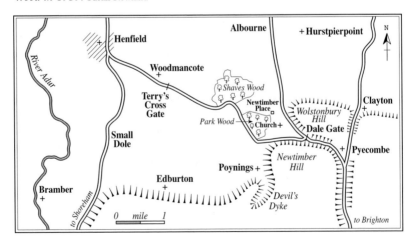

booty consisted of some £20[2] in cash, a £5 Brighton Union Bank note, a cheque for £13 and a gold watch, which had been wrenched from the victim's neck, to which it had been attached by a gold chain. The only coins found in the dead man's pockets by the police were three halfpence, although in a pocket in the sleeve of his coat three sixpences, a fourpenny piece and a penny were found. The gig had been turned back in its tracks and was discovered at Poynings. There it was found to have the mounting step wrenched round, which would have required great force.

The news from Kirton and the Hodsons of the killing reached the police headquarters at Brighton Town Hall at 4 o'clock on Wednesday. A great number of people, many of them personal friends of Mr Griffith, visited the murder scene, which was about seven miles from Brighton. Captain Mackay, Chief Officer of the East Sussex Constabulary, took horse immediately on hearing of the murder and rode to the spot, having previously instructed his superintendent to spread officers in various directions. Mr Chase, the Chief Officer of the Brighton Police, also dispatched Mr White, Mr Barnden (whom we shall meet again) and some of his most active and efficient officers to different locations but no clue to the perpetrator(s) of the murder was ever discovered. This was despite the offer of a very substantial reward of £300 and a free pardon to an accomplice for information leading to the conviction of the culprit(s).

The inquest on George Griffith was held in two sessions at the *Plough* public house in Pycombe, situated about a mile from the spot where the murder was committed. Throughout the day, the premises were packed with visitors from Brighton attending in an official and unofficial capacity. They included Somers Clarke (the family solicitor and Clerk to the Brighton Vestry from 1830 to 1892), Harry Mills Blaker (Griffith's medical attendant and an intimate family friend), S Platt, Sewell and several Brighton tradesmen.

Blaker confirmed that death was caused by the single shot through the chest and would have been almost instantaneous. The bullet, which differed from those carried by Griffith, penetrated the heart and finally lodged in the back of it. The clothes were singed and the flesh scorched and the firearm had evidently been fired close to the victim's breast.

The verdict reached was 'Murder by persons unknown'.

---

2. Remarkably, the purchasing power of this sum in today's values is approximately £1200.

On Monday, 12 February 1849, Griffith was buried in the new Cemetery in Brighton, where a vault had been duly prepared. The Commissioners of Brighton attended, anxious to show their respect for the deceased, who had been at an active member of their body. The procession was accompanied by a large concourse of people. In the words of the *Brighton Gazette*:

> *The scene was of more than the usually painful character, owing to the peculiar and melancholy circumstances by which the deceased met his death.*

In *Sussex in Bygone Days* (1919), Nathaniel Paine Blaker MRCS, wrote about the case as a boyhood memory. He described a curious sequel to the crime:

> *Years after when some workmen were cleaning out the mud from a pond close to the road along which the murdered man had passed, and about a mile to the East of Terry's Lodge, a man who was walking by called out to them that they would find Mr Griffith's watch if they searched carefully; this they did, found it and brought it to Mr Somers Clark, he being solicitor to the Griffith family.*

This incident, according to Lewis T Ackerman (*Sussex County Magazine*, 1952), occurred seven years after the crime. But one wonders: how could this helpful passer-by have possessed the knowledge he did, and why were more details not taken about him and recorded? It is surprising no one's suspicions were aroused.

Other questions in this strange affair are why the murdering thief should have flung the watch away at all, for he was not being pursued. The fact that he wore a mask could have meant that he feared recognition by someone he knew, namely William Martin, to whom the warning letter had been addressed. But why even warn anybody, and thereby put them on the alert? Another point to ponder is that the clasp knife was left at the scene of the crime, yet it was a moonlit night. The assailant must have felt unhurried otherwise he would not have delayed to turn the horse and gig round.

One H F Squire wrote a letter to the editor of the *Sussex County Magazine* which was published in the November 1952 issue. It referred to Ackerman's account and reads as follows:

Without presuming to solve the mystery, here are a few additional details which were given to me by an old local inhabitant some months ago, and which I believe have never been published. I am not including names.

There was a farm worker, we will call him X, living in one of a pair of cottages. On the evening of Mr Griffith's call at the White Hart, *X was in the bar with several of his friends. On seeing Mr Griffith arrive, he got up, paid up, and went out. This was so unusual at that early hour, that it caused much ribald comment.*

The next page of the story concerns X's wife. She was an invalid and was extremely worried because her husband was out so late at night; in fact he had not returned by midnight. In the early hours of the morning, however, she heard the heavy tread of her husband as he came up the flagstones towards the cottage. He stopped and fumbled at the well, then came round to the back-door. Their mutual conversation remains a mystery. It was noticed later that X produced golden guineas to pay for his drinks for some considerable period.

These facts were never brought to light during the enquiry, due either to village clannishness, or fear of smugglers' reprisals. The sequel, however, is interesting. In course of time, X died, and the cottages were pulled down to make way for a small house, in which my informant and her mother came to live.

Many times, they have during the night heard the heavy tramp of labourers' boots walk round the house to the back-door, and then – nothing. They have even opened the door, but there was no-one there. When they moved, a clergyman and his wife took up their residence in the same house. My informant asked him one day if he had ever heard any footsteps. 'Quite often,' he replied, 'but don't tell my wife. She would be scared.'

Chapter 4

Horror in Balcombe Tunnel
1881

Ambition ... has been my ruin, an evil now coupled with a fearful habit of deception ... No one gets wicked at all at once, they go step by step, the road daily becomes more easy until at last they can go no further but find themselves engulfed for eternity in the awful ruin of everlasting death.

(Percy Lefroy Mapleton, November 1881)

Frederick Isaac Gold was a man of habit. A former stockbroker, little more than sixty years of age, he had lived at 13 Clermont Terrace, Preston, Brighton – see top of map on page 147 – for ten years prior to the summer of 1881 when this drama unfolds. Although he had retired from business eighteen years before, having owned a corn chandler's shop in Walworth, among other shrewd investments, he had by no means given up moneymaking entirely.

He was somewhat miserly, a characteristic inevitably accompanied by anxiety and worries. He had a great fear of anyone getting into his bedroom at night and thus always locked the door. Except when on his way to the bank with the weekly takings, he never carried more than a handful of silver. He was 'close' in money matters, even with his wife.

Physically, he was robust. In defence of any money he had on his person, he would be doubly so. Yet in normal circumstances, as Mrs Gold later testified, 'He was of a very timid disposition. At the least thing he got nervous.'

He usually travelled to London on Monday mornings to attend to some investments he had made there, returning by the 2.10 pm train, which arrived at Preston Park at 3.30. It was a journey he hated because it brought him into contact with strangers. Indeed his fear and suspicion of them was so great as to be almost obsessive. Being convinced that people were prying into his affairs and afraid of being tricked into giving them information, he would usually pretend to be asleep to discourage fellow passengers from talking to him.

This ploy could, of course, work two ways. Supposing he, a prosperous-looking gentleman, was apparently deep in slumber and the only other occupant of the compartment was desperate for money? Supposing that person – armed with a revolver and knife – had boarded the train for the specific purpose of ending his financial problems? Such was the scenario on the sweltering afternoon of 27 June 1881.

That other person was 'Arthur' Lefroy, aged 22, a failed author, journalist and actor from Wallington, Carshalton, Surrey. Ambitious, vain and greedy, a petty thief, prone to mood swings, and quite brazen and plausible when the occasion demanded, he was physically no match for his heavier-built victim. Only 5 feet 8 inches tall, he was a gangling, very slight figure of a man in a shabby genteel frock coat, whose thinness made him seem taller than he was. The previous Christmas he had dropped the family name of Mapleton in favour of his second name, Lefroy, which he thought more 'select' and easier on the ear, for he was planning to write for the stage. For the same reason, he had abandoned his Christian name, Percy. He did possess some social skills, as an ex-colleague writing to the *Daily Telegraph* was later to record:

> *Lefroy had a habit of ingratiating himself that was remarkable, and in conversation possessed a power of narrative that was essentially dramatic, not to say sensational. In the presence of strangers he was polite and respectful, and his general bearing was such as to produce a favourable impression.*

His efforts to mix with polite society and join the theatrical and literary set had, however, almost bankrupted him. His cousin and landlord, Mr T G Clayton, and Mr Seale, another cousin, were pressing for repayment of loans and pledges. It was time to find a solution.

He was the owner of a small-calibre revolver, which, under the name of Lee, he had pledged with Messrs Adams and Helstead, pawnbrokers in the Borough, on 21 June. In desperation, he had redeemed his pledge on the morning of the 27 June – a few hours before the crime – and travelled to London Bridge. There, with the little money he had left, he bought the first-class single ticket to Brighton which he firmly believed would enable him to turn his fortunes around.

His first choice of victim, he later wrote, was unsuitable although he did notice 'an old gentleman getting into a carriage some way down the train.' The man in the compartment seemed to sense Lefroy's evil intention:

... he was looking steadily at me ... and his eyes seemed to pass into my soul. I could stand it no longer and got out of the compartment, my companion little thinking that to his inquisitive looks he probably owed his life.

Lefroy got out at East Croydon and walked past all the carriages, looking in at the windows to see if any first class passenger was by himself. He came across Gold, the perfect victim. Lefroy realised the shooting would have to take place somewhere noisier than usual. Merstham Tunnel was ideal. He described what happened:

Mr Gold ... was then sitting uneasily in the middle seat with his back to the engine, I nearly in front of him, facing the engine in the near corner. When the train started, Mr Gold was looking out of the window and I was ostensibly reading the paper. On, on through the dear familiar scenery rushed the train, reminding me, had I been really there, of many and many a cherished walk with those I loved. But of none of those things was I thinking now, as I sat there with fixed and staring eyes, my hand slowly drawing the deadly weapon from its hiding place. Every minute of waiting seemed an hour. We were dashing now through Stoats Nest and I knew that soon the yawning gulf of blackness would be upon us. The pistol was now in my right hand, loaded, cocked and <u>levelled</u>. Oh God! How can I write what follows? Quicker and quicker fled the train, higher and higher rose the chalky walls on either side, and fiercer and fiercer raged a battle in my head not yet long commenced, but which, in these few seconds, was to decide my earthly fate for ever. Which was it to be, a pistol, money and happiness? Or innocence and all my false and hollow life laid bare? Quick, no time for reflection. Higher and higher rose the walls of chalk, shutting out all sight of heaven and telling me that now I must decide for once, for ever. Nearer and nearer, closer and closer, the yawning mouth was close upon us. Fifty yards, thirty, ten, 5, we were in! I closed my eyes, extended my arm and fired and as the trigger fell the engine gave an awful shriek, like the last bitter cry of my good spirit.... As the report died away I sprang to my feet and peered into the gloom where my offending victim had been sitting. Had I killed him?

The shots were heard by a number of people on the train, but because they were inexplicable they were ignored, or put down to fog detonators. The latter was the surprising conjecture of Guard Walters – surprising when one bears in mind it was a bright and hot summer's day. William Gibson, a chemist from Brighton, explained to his young son, already frightened by the sudden darkness of the tunnel, that the noises were 'only fog signals', although he himself did have his doubts. The driver and fireman, overwhelmed by the din of their locomotive at speed in a confined environment, were understandably to report that they 'never heard a thing.'

Lefroy had not killed Gold:

> *... in an instant he was upon me, not before, though, in my madness I had discharged three or four more shots at him. Oh merciful Father give me strength to finish now. In an instant I was extended on the ground up against the furthest door, keeping at bay as well as I could the justly infuriated man, who with one hand grasped me by the throat and with the other struck me savagely upon the head with the revolver, which he grasped by the handle, striking me with the end of the muzzle. Not a word was uttered and there in the darkness of the tunnel that death struggle commenced. The awful blackness of the tunnel without, the air laden with the fearful smell of powder, the half gloom of that living grave, only made visible by the feeble light above which shed its sickly light upon the livid face that fiercely looked in mine, made such a fearful impression on me that never, if I live a thousand years, could I forget it. Poor Mr Gold, who might have been unwounded for any effect it had upon him and then could easily have pulled the communicator a dozen times, had he wished to do so, never appeared to think of it. As for me, I was a child in his hands and I had as much as I could do to save myself from being throttled when he threw the pistol on one side and went to grasp my throat with both his hands. But the train sped on, and our positions never changed, he pinioning me to the ground, while I as strenuously resisted, neither being armed and both being on the floor of the carriage ...*

There was supposedly a witness – albeit a long-range one – to the early stage of the struggle. A Mrs Brown, of King's Head Cottage, Horley, had been looking out of the window of her cottage when the 2.10 roared by. For the briefest moment, she and her young daughter caught a glimpse of two men standing up in a first-class carriage, apparently fighting. Dismissing what they had seen at first as men 'only larking', they did inform the police when Lefroy was later being sought in connection with the crime. However, Lefroy refuted her testimony:

> *Never once was there any "scuffling or fighting" standing up, from the time the first shot was fired until within a few miles of Balcombe.*

Top: *Interior and exterior views of a cottage at Horley from which a witness saw a train passing with two men struggling in a carriage.* Centre: *The entrance to Balcombe Tunnel.* Bottom: *The spot in the tunnel where Gold's body was found. The house in Cathcart Road, Wallington, where Lefroy lodged.* Hulton Archive

Mrs Brown and her daughter must be either greatly mistaken as to the train, or telling a wilful falsehood. At last the sense of the deadly struggle changed. All at once, as if by mutual agreement, we released each other, both maddened with fury and <u>both</u> believing they were fighting for their lives.... I knew that if we <u>both</u> arrived at Brighton, my fate was sealed, and I did not know but what we might be quite close there ... And now before Gold could prevent me I had sprung up and throwing open the door called to him in a voice of some demon fresh from Hell below that made me start and tremble when I heard it, to jump from the train or I'd shoot him, at the same time snatching up the pistol. And then with the train flying along at fifty miles an hour, the door wide open and the floor already slippery with blood, the awful ending came. A mad refusal ... backwards and forwards, turning and twisting, blade against pistol, another whistle from the engine, black, bitter darkness, a sudden jerk, an awful cry, a door quickly shut and I found myself alone.

Yet he was not alone. Hordes of demons with bloody faces and grinning imps peopled the compartment, bleeding hands attacking his throat time after time, feverish voices and wild despairing cries were heard like some mighty chorus to their song of murder and cracking pistol shots sounded in that gloomy blackness – a blackness with a crimson tinge filled with furious beings trying to pull him out of the carriage and down to hell.

He gathered his senses and realised he must dispose, of the various articles left by Mr Gold in the carriage. The first thing he hurled out was the revolver, which fell in some underwood close to a bridge not very far from the tunnel. On the floor was his victim's watch, with a small piece of chain attached to it, while on the seat where he had been sitting was his handkerchief. Lefroy, fearing he might be searched, hastily slipped the watch into his shoe. Gold's purse was found to contain barely half a sovereign:

This then was my gold mine, the harvest that was reward for my guilty act, an old fashioned watch and ten shillings! As I put the empty purse in my pocket there slowly came into my mind those awful words 'What shall it profit a man if he gain the <u>whole world</u> and lose his own soul?'

Somehow it seemed to him that his bloodstained collar would attract more attention than anything else, so he hastily took it off and cast it from the window. He was just congratulating himself that he had got rid of everything when, to his horror, he saw Gold's umbrella lying in the rack. He was about to throw it out of the window when he felt the train perceptibly slackening speed. Terrified in case it might be Brighton, he put his head out to find a brief halt was being made at Hassocks Gate. He was about to alight and flee but before he could do so, the train moved off 'and soon was flying along as fast as ever.' In despair, he decided he would make a clean breast of the whole thing at Brighton, but a minute after entering Clayton Tunnel he changed this intention to a resolve to fight for his life even to the bitter end in the coming ordeal at the station.

A strong force of labourers was subsequently ordered by the London, Brighton and South Coast Railway company to search the track between Croydon and Preston. No fewer than a dozen men were assigned to the narrow stretch between Balcombe Tunnel and the Ouse Viaduct, to the south of Balcombe Station.

One find was Lefroy's bloodstained shirt collar. Ten miles south of the spot where Gold's body was discovered, the hat the victim had worn, similarly bloodstained, was picked up. His blood-soaked umbrella was found at the side of the track, fully twenty miles from where the hat had been found and well south of Hassocks Station.

When Lefroy stumbled, covered in blood, from the compartment in the second coach behind the engine at Preston Park Station, he asked the man who opened the door if he could see a doctor. He told Collector Gibson he had been murderously attacked and he was taken to see Station Master Hall.

The story Lefroy recounted was that there had been two other men in the compartment when he entered it at London Bridge.

Preston Park Station, the first station north of Brighton. Here Lefroy alighted bloodstained and dishevelled from the London Bridge train. Author's collection

One of them was a prosperous-looking gentleman in his late fifties while the other was rough-looking and had whiskers. He was 'probably a countryman'. Neither had spoken to him or to each other. When the train had entered Merstham Tunnel he heard a loud report and at the same time received a violent blow on the head. He remembered nothing after that until, bleeding profusely, he recovered consciousness on the floor of the compartment. His fellow-travellers had disappeared.

Repeating the story to Station Master Hall, Lefroy embellished it by saying that he had been hit on the head and shot by the countryman. Both Hall and Gibson, however, wondered where the two missing men could have got off the train. Lefroy was greatly alarmed by Guard Watson picking the watch by the chain up from his shoe and asking him how it got there, to which he replied that he knew nothing about it. The guard then placed it on the seat by Lefroy's side and left him.

Stationmaster Hall finally decided to send the injured man, escorted by Gibson, to the stationmaster at Brighton, Mr Anscombe, requesting him to arrange for a medical examination. Lefroy began enjoying all the attention but was not so keen to report to the police. He recovered from his supposed state of shock rapidly enough and his chief concern seemed to be where he could obtain replacements for his collar and tie.

In company with Watson and Gibson, he was taken from the Superintendent's Office to the police headquarters at the Town

Brighton Station in the 1870s, from a local directory. Author's collection

Hall. While there, he was aghast to discover that he still had in his possession the razor he had set out with that morning and Mr Gold's purse. These he disposed of down a lavatory pipe, while his police escort stared dutifully for five minutes at the closet door.

Duly searched despite his protestations, Lefroy told his interrogators that the reason for his visit to Brighton was to discuss with Mrs Nye Chart – the manageress of the prestigious Theatre Royal and Opera House – a play he had written for production in her theatre. Mrs Chart's local standing and influence were such as to change the attitude of the police towards him. Offering a generous reward for his assailant's capture put him in an even better light with them.

When taken to the County Hospital, his 'wild-eyed' appearance initially caused surgeon Bernard Hall to believe him insane. As far as the marks on his patient's face and hands were concerned, he had never before seen anything like them. It was, he thought, possible that the six small semicircular cuts upon his scalp could have been caused by a pistol or revolver pressed against his head. This assessment, together with the finding of two revolver bullets in the train compartment – one in the seat cushions and one wedged into the woodwork near the communication cord – lent added credibility to Lefroy's version of events.

The police handling of this case would later be the subject of some criticism on two counts. Firstly their lack of logical enquiry at Brighton and secondly the ineptitude of Detective Sergeant George Holmes, the officer selected to escort Lefroy home. He had served for eleven years in the Metropolitan force and had been seconded to the LBSCR to supplement the modest staff of that company.

In Brighton, for example, no surprise was expressed when Lefroy insisted on returning to London forthwith on account of urgent and pressing business awaiting him. Yet he had only left there an hour and a half before and had – strangely – made the journey on a single ticket.

And what of the interview with Mrs Chart? The police failed to make any enquiries with her about Lefroy and his credentials. Yet they did at least consider that his movements should be monitored and insisted that he be escorted on his journey home, despite his protests that he could now fend for himself.

Holmes and his ward caught the 6.10 pm from Brighton. In a neighbouring siding, sightseers were watching the team checking over the carriage Lefroy had travelled in.

Less than two hours earlier, halfway up the London line, Ganger Thomas Jennings and his nephew, William, had made a gruesome discovery. When the men first entered the cool, mile-long, Balcombe Tunnel, they were relieved to escape the glare of the afternoon sun. At 4.30 Tom's naphtha light cast a glow over what appeared to be a shapeless heap of clothes between the up and down lines. Closer inspection revealed the bloodied, battered body of Gold, his face upturned to the tunnel roof. His left fist was dug into the ballast and his right arm lay across his chest as though in self-defence. A broken gold watch-chain was around his neck.

The railwaymen quickly left the tunnel to report their find. Balcombe signal box was alerted via a platelayer, Stephen Williams, and from there the message was telegraphed to London. There was some delay in London Bridge being granted permission to relay the signal to other stations along the line. Even worse, Brighton – the southern headquarters of the company's police – was not contacted at all.

Thomas and William Jennings, together with William's father, helped to escort the dead Mr Gold to the *Railway Inn* in Balcombe village, where the body was placed in a small adjoining brick shed. Thomas, with a policeman, then went back to search the tunnel. There they found two 'flash sovereigns' similar to those found in Lefroy's possession. These were worthless 'To Hanover' brass counters depicting the Duke of Cumberland riding off to that city, sword at the ready and wearing a tiny crown.

Gold's body, duly examined, presented a dreadful sight. His face was black with the dirt of the footway between the tracks but also appeared to have been scorched by explosive powder from a shot fired at point-blank range. There were knife wounds in the cheeks and hands and the point of a knife had seemingly also caused a semi-circular and blood-encrusted wound disfiguring the mouth, extending from one side of the chin to the other. There were fourteen knife cuts in all and a three-inch wound in the back of the head which was open down to the bone.

A local doctor reported that death had resulted from haemorrhage, caused by a violent blow delivered by a blunt instrument, or perhaps by the dead man's fall from the train. It was later confirmed he had been shot, for a bullet the size of a pea was found in the second vertebra of his neck. It had travelled from a wound near the eye.

The victim's widow had naturally become concerned when her husband had failed to return home. She assumed at first that he had been detained on business, but by the time the 8.15 had been and gone with no sign of him, she walked down to Preston Park

Station to inquire if there had been an accident. Unaccountably, the station-master – who had earlier encountered Lefroy – actually allayed her fears, stating that all was normal on the line.

Only at ten o'clock did she receive a telegram from Balcombe informing her of the finding of her husband's body nearly six hours before. Because of a slip-up by the Post Office, the delivery of the telegram had been delayed.

It was not until nearly midnight that the train conveying the infuriated and grief-stricken widow made its special stop at Balcombe. Mrs Gold, however, was to prove to be in no state to view her husband's body. That grim duty fell on a Mr James Hollis, who had accompanied her. She was, however, to be of invaluable help in the enquiry in the matter of the make and appearance of her husband's missing watch. She was able to provide a detailed description: it was gold, and on its white face was printed the name of its maker: Griffiths, Mile End Road.

This was a breakthrough for the railway police, and they immediately followed up the clue. They knew that this could well be the link they needed between Lefroy and his victim.

News of the body's discovery had been passed on to Holmes earlier by the station-master of Three Bridges Station when the 6.10 stopped at Balcombe. Holmes was also warned to keep a close eye on Lefroy. Not long before, the aspiring playwright had been in a relaxed and cheerful mood recounting his extraordinary experiences of that afternoon when the train left Brighton.

The officer and his charge eventually arrived in normally sleepy Wallington, where Lefroy had been lodging for three months with the Claytons at 4 Cathcart Road. Mrs Clayton ran a small children's nursery on the premises. Later the innocent couple were to be driven out of their home – and indeed away from the district altogether – by numerous and disruptive visits from police and detectives and by the public's reaction to their association with Lefroy.

Tonight, the Claytons were understandably surprised when their lodger returned unexpectedly – doubly so when they saw him in the company of a police officer. They were also concerned to see that young Arthur, who had impressed them with his (supposed) theatrical and social connections, had been injured. At this stage, of course, they knew nothing of the incident which had taken place.

They thus had no reason to doubt the young man's version of events and were relieved to hear Holmes' explanation that he was acting as Lefroy's bodyguard to ensure he came to no harm before producing his evidence to Scotland Yard.

Armed with full details of the watch, meanwhile, the police in Croydon were asked to contact Holmes. In an initial telegram, he was alerted to the importance of this item in Lefroy's possession. The number was crucial.

Holmes proceeded in surprisingly leisurely fashion. After a social chat with the Claytons, he finally asked Lefroy what the number on the watch was. On being told it was 56,312, Holmes checked the watch and found that it was 16,261. Unbelievably, he told Lefroy he was mistaken and that it was 16,261 ... Lefroy's nonchalant reaction was that he had forgotten the number. Holmes also unquestioningly accepted Lefroy's statement that he did not know the maker's name since he had bought it off a friend. The officer failed even to enquire who the friend was.

When asked where he could be found next day, Lefroy casually responded: 'Wallington, up to 12. After that at the United Arts Club, Savoy Street, Strand.' Whereupon he saw Holmes out.

Lefroy recalled:

The instant the detective went I ran upstairs, changed my clothes, said goodbye to my cousin, had something to eat and <u>fully twenty minutes</u> after Holmes had gone I went softly out at the front gate (there being no one in sight) and turned my back weary and sick at heart upon the dear old place for ever.

Only when he reached Wallington Station and received the second telegram, advising him of the make and number of Gold's watch, did Holmes realise the opportunity he had missed. When he returned to the house, the bird had flown.

In the grey overcoat the wanted man had left behind in Cathcart Road were pawn tickets relating to items pledged, under the assumed names 'Lee' and also 'Leigh', at no fewer than four different pawnbrokers in districts extending from the West End to Croydon.

Early in the afternoon following Lefroy's escape, 'Wanted for Murder' police notices giving a concise description of the man and details of the watch began appearing at virtually every public location. A week later, on 4 July, Scotland Yard issued a new notice, this time offering a substantial reward of £200 for information. Half of this sum was contributed by the railway.

Lefroy, meanwhile, wandered around the capital, having walked from Wallington to London via Thornton Heath, Streatham and Kennington. He arrived at the *Sussex Hotel*, Bouverie Street, off Fleet Street, about 1 am, where he slept for the night in the name of 'Lee'. All next day he was wandering about Victoria Park, but at night walked down to Blackfriars and slept at a coffee house near the bridge. The following day he spent on Blackheath and in Greenwich Park, returning at night to London. He threw Mr Gold's watch over the middle arch of Blackfriars Bridge and slept at a coffee tavern near the obelisk.

On the Thursday, he took up lodgings, under the assumed name of Clark, at 32 Smith Street, Stepney, in the establishment of a widow by the name of Bickers. The rent of 6s per week suited him and he paid in advance. He told the landlady he was an engraver, just down from Liverpool, and that his luggage would be following. He made a favourable impression on her, for in later years she remembered him as 'a nice young man, very pale and delicate-looking'. She was nevertheless reluctant to leave him alone in her house. A couple of times she mentioned the Brighton line murder to him, for it was in all the papers, but Lefroy's response was vague and uninterested.

The *Daily Telegraph* made newspaper history by obtaining and publishing Lefroy's picture while for its part, the Yard produced a pen and ink portrait to supplement its previous description – and also printed the facsimile of a recent letter written by Lefroy in case anyone recognised the handwriting. A police watch was mounted on all trains for the continent and all shipping leaving the Channel ports. The Home Office even offered a pardon to any accomplice – who had not actually committed the murder – coming forward with vital information.

Widow Bickers had a certain pride in her house – after all, 'Mr Clark's' predecessor had lodged there for three years – so her feelings on seeing it described in the papers, some days later, as 'a dingy lodging house in the squalid East End', may be imagined.

The new lodger, unsurprisingly, rarely emerged from his room. After a week, as predicted by the police, he broke cover – not by showing himself in public but by having a telegram sent. The addressee was his cousin and

The Wanted/Reward Notice for Lefroy, reproducing his handwriting as a further identifying feature. Author's collection

fellow-lodger in Wallington, Mr Seale, at a firm in Gresham Street in the City. Pleading a twisted ankle, Lefroy persuaded a neighbouring greengrocer, one Mr Doyle, to take the message to the post office for him (having unsuccessfully asked the allegedly busy Mrs Bickers to do so). It requested that his wages be brought to him that evening at about seven. Doyle was given sixpence for his trouble.

On the evening of Friday 8 July, two armed and determined CID inspectors, Donald Swanson and Frederick Jarvis, swooped on the lodgings in Smith Street. Jarvis kept guard outside the building while Swanson charged up the stairs to the first-floor landing. As he hurled open the bedroom door, he ducked to one side, flattening himself against the adjoining wall. For all he knew, Lefroy might well open fire on him. There was no shot, no struggle. Confirming his identity, a dispirited, almost relieved, Arthur Lefroy said from the semi-darkness within, 'I was expecting you.' 'I am arresting you', responded Swanson, 'on the charge of murdering Mr Frederick Gold.'

Allowing the handcuffs to be slipped on, a pale and drawn Lefroy declared 'I am not obliged to make any reply, and I don't think I shall do so.' He said the same to Jarvis when he entered the room and repeated the charge. Lefroy then added: 'Well, I will qualify that by saying I am not guilty.'

Lying even now, Lefroy denied he had been given a key to a chest of drawers in the room. There was one drawer that was locked and he claimed it was 'impossible to move'. Jarvis forced it open and in it found a black cloth waistcoat and a black scarf stained with blood. The other drawers contained two cloth caps, a false moustache, a pair of false whiskers to hook over the ears, and a pair of scissors. These were Lefroy's own and had been used to cut off his moustache and whiskers.

In the closed cab on the way to the police station, Lefroy told Swanson how he regretted having run away and was pleased to have been tracked down:

> *I am glad you found me for I was sick and tired of it all. I should have given myself up in a day or two, but I could not bear the exposure.*

Mrs Bickers' sensitivities about her establishment were soon to be soothed by a relative securing for her 15 per cent of the reward for Lefroy's capture. By having doubts about 'Clark' and sending her daughter to Gresham Street to check whether someone of that name really worked there, she had greatly helped the police.

By the following month, she had moved to Jamaica Street off the Commercial Road.

At the police station, Lefroy repeatedly said how relieved he was. 'I was really wretched, I had nothing to eat all day', he told the officers. He did, however, ask to see a lawyer. It was also plain that, despite his relief, he was glad he would not be seeing any of his 'so-called friends from Wallington', meaning Seale.

Swanson and Jarvis were chosen to escort the prisoner by rail to Lewes Gaol the day after the arrest. Just as on the journey with Holmes, Lefroy appeared relaxed, smoking and chatting with his captors. He lost his composure just once – as the train began approaching Balcombe Tunnel. Increasingly agitated, he was in such a state by the time it passed through the tunnel itself that he was unable to speak. At Haywards Heath, where the trio had to change trains for Lewes, a group of passengers who had learned Lefroy was coming hooted and jeered at them. Others soon joined in. It was a struggle in all the commotion for the officers to reach the Lewes train and, with help from the station staff, bundle their prisoner aboard. On their arrival at Lewes, a prison van awaited Lefroy, who had seemed unperturbed by the demonstration up the line and continued to appear so.

★ ★ ★

His trial, before Lord Chief Justice Coleridge at the Maidstone Assizes, began on Friday 4 November 1881. Attorney General, Sir Henry James, later Lord James of Hertford, led for the prosecution. Defending Lefroy was the noted barrister, Mr Montagu Williams, who was to make a courageous, but ultimately unsuccessful, plea on his client's behalf.

The courtroom was packed. It was so crowded outside that access to the building was difficult. Many bystanders had journeyed from London on a special excursion ticket. Strangely, however, there were far fewer people on the second day, the pavement outside the court being almost deserted.

Ever-vain, Lefroy wanted to look elegant in court. His request to redeem his frock coat from pawn was turned down but his warders did allow him to carry his topper, his latest acquisition. At times, he gave more attention to admiring that item than to following the proceedings.

Despite some discrepancies in the evidence of certain witnesses, which were duly fastened on by the defence, the case against Lefroy grew inexorably. His position was further undermined by the many contradictions in his statements. He

An artist's impression drawn from the press gallery at Maidstone Assizes of the trial of Percy Lefroy Mapleton. Hulton Archive

told the court he could remember nothing except a loud explosion. Two other passengers had, he said, been present in the carriage. One had attacked him with a gouge (this later became 'a revolver'), then both men had assaulted him before 'getting out on to the road.' At Preston Park, and again at Brighton, he had declared he knew nothing about the flash sovereigns, yet he had lamely replied, after the police had found two similar coins in his clothing, 'I suppose I must have got them playing at whist!'

Far from impartial, Judge Coleridge set himself against Lefroy, both during the first day of the trial and on Saturday when it ended. Montagu Williams bravely argued that the inconsistencies in his client's account of events were due to him still being confused by the effects of the 'assault'. His later escape from Cathcart Road was simply the nervous reaction of an imaginative young man alarmed by continuous questioning. Daringly, the counsel scornfully described the prosecution case as resting on largely circumstantial evidence. His arguments were admittedly plausible, as when he asked:

> *Is it probable that a man who meant to commit murder would prelude it by a fraud, and equip himself with visiting cards giving his true name and address? And why, if he had that morning redeemed a pistol from the pawnbrokers – redeemed it with the intention of employing it in his crime – should he have carried pawnbroking duplicates in his pockets?*

Nor was there an atom of evidence that Lefroy, as the prosecution claimed, had been 'looking from carriage to carriage for his victim.' As for the 'third man', why should he not have existed?

And why could he not have murdered Gold, stunned Lefroy and left the train when it had slowed to a mere crawl at Hassocks Gate?

Although Williams succeeded in reducing some members of the jury to tears, the Lord Chief Justice soon righted the balance. Contrasting Frederick Gold with Arthur Lefroy, he highlighted how different the latter was by pointing out:

> *He is without money, curiously erratic in his habits, not scrupulous in regard to honesty, and of his early life, how brought up, and in company with what associates, we know nothing.*

His lengthy summing-up set out the facts fairly but was heavily weighted against the prisoner. Even Lefroy himself began to sit up and take notice. For him, this could be the beginning of the end. The damning evidence against the hypothesised departure from the 2.10 of a 'third man' was the discovery of the murdered man's umbrella well south of that point – much nearer to Brighton. It could only have been jettisoned by the murderer.

The jury took only ten minutes to reach their 'Guilty' verdict.

After the death sentence had been passed on him, Lefroy, true to character, turned towards the jury box and said

> *Gentlemen of the jury, some day, when too late, you will learn that you have murdered me.*

Just under three weeks later, on 29 November, Percy Lefroy Mapleton was hanged at Lewes Gaol. He did confess then that his pose as the persecuted innocent had been false, but he had never intended to murder Mr Gold.

Outside the precincts, a restrained crowd waited for the black flag to be hoisted, signalling that the hanging had taken place. The great

Lord Chief Justice Coleridge was decidedly unsympathetic to Lefroy.
Author's collection

bell of the prison (never before used for an execution) began to toll. The sun, dispelling the cold, early-morning mist, shone brilliantly from out of a cloudless blue sky. 'At exactly nine o'clock', reported the *Sussex Express*, 'the trap was heard to fall ... and slowly, but quietly, the bystanders started to make their way home.'

True justice was indeed served on that cold November morning in 1881. Yet before his death, Lefroy placed the following on record:

I am deeply sensible of the Christian charity of Mrs Gold for extending to me under such circumstances her free forgiveness for the wrong which I have done her ... Had I ten thousand lives I would give them willingly to bring poor Mr Gold once more to life. As that however is beyond my power I can only humbly confess my fault and ask forgiveness of Almighty God.

A TOXIC DEMISE

CHAPTER 5

Poison by Prescription
1866

By the light of a couple of police lanterns, the coffin was hastily lowered into the earth.

Miss Charlotte Landsell, the owner of 36 Bedford Square, Brighton, was favourably impressed by her new tenants, a doctor and his wife. Married for only five months, Alfred and Ellen Warder had taken up furnished rooms there, not far from the sea, on 23 May 1866.

Dr Warder seemed very professional and had, indeed, achieved some distinction in his chosen career, being an expert in toxicology. Miss Landsell was probably unaware that he had been a lecturer on poisons at the Grosvenor Place School of Medicine in London, or that he had been one of the school of doctors who had given evidence in defence of the notorious poisoner, Palmer. It is also unlikely that she knew that this was his third marriage.

In fact, it was only later that she would also learn that the genteel doctor's first two wives had met their deaths in suspicious circumstances ...

Mrs Warder, 36 years of age, did not strike Miss Landsell as strong, but she certainly did not – at first – seem ill. She had married without the knowledge of any of her family. Her brother, Richard Branwell, who lived in nearby Cambridge Road, Hove, must by then have accepted the union and no doubt imagined it would last for many years. He, too, was one of the medical fraternity, being a well-known local surgeon. The last thing he would have imagined would be having to visit his sister in a professional capacity.

The couple had not been settled in their rooms for long before Ellen Warder became so unwell that her brother anxiously called in the widely-respected Dr R P B Taafe, (who would two years later found the Brighton Hospital for Sick Children at 178 Western Road). Yet the medicine he prescribed failed to restore the patient. Prior to that time, her husband had been treating her.

Bedford Square from the promenade. The Warders lodged about halfway up the right-hand side. Chris Horlock collection

He would tell later of his wife's hysterical attacks, how she had complained that she was constantly having to pass urine, and suffered severe pains in the bladder. When he first attended the patient, he had been giving her twenty drop doses of Fleming's Tincture of Aconite, as the only remedy to allay the pain.

For his part, Dr Taaafe objected to both the remedy and the dose, and had instead substituted henbane, tincture of castor, valerian, laudanum, and water fomentations.

These seemed to do the patient good. He also prescribed valerianate of zinc. After some days, however, Dr Warder told him his wife had become tired of these remedies and could no longer take them. This he said in Mrs Warder's presence, adding that she was now vomiting twice a day. Her stomach was resisting the medicines and drugs, which she could not keep down.

Dr Taafe then stopped giving her these remedies and instead prescribed effervescing saline draughts and aromatic spirit of ammonia containing chloric ether. He also substituted simple saline draughts with one minimum dose of prussic acid. When he wrote out the prescription he arranged with Dr Warder to have the doses made up.

36 Bedford Square, where Dr Warder and his wife had furnished apartments. The author

Yet the sickness got worse. Dr Taafe saw Mrs Warder take a draught of medicine which she brought up five minutes later. She complained of griping pains in the stomach and then felt compelled to spit saliva, which made Dr Taafe wonder whether she might be pregnant. He came to the conclusion, however, that she was not.

The vomiting and pains nevertheless continued, which mystified him. He prescribed sub-carbonate of bismuth and solid opium, which appeared to relieve her. Yet fresh symptoms appeared. Her tongue begun swelling up, its covering being white and sodden. Dr Warder's explanation, again in his wife's presence, was that she had drunk a cup of scalding hot fluid.

When Dr Taafe visited on Saturday, June 30, he was so shocked by Ellen Warder's appearance that he suggested to Mr Branwell that further medical aid and a nurse should be called in. He felt it would be better if Mrs Warder were left alone for a few days without visitors – even her husband.

The next morning, an anxious Mr Branwell called at the house at 5.30 and found his sister dead. He was puzzled by the death and could not understand the cause. He left a note later in the morning for Dr Taafe, who saw him that afternoon. Taafe later stated:

Mr Branwell looked at me very hard, said he had a painful impression in his own mind, and that he intended to mention it to me, but from motives of delicacy had not done so.

On examining her, Taafe was not satisfied that her death was natural. Even though he conducted a post-mortem with the assistance of two other doctors (the highly-experienced Dr Withers Moore and Mr Jowers, a surgeon) in the presence of Dr Warder, the cause of death could not be discovered. He therefore refused to sign the death certificate, which meant an inquest had to be held.

The proceedings were conducted by the Brighton coroner, David Black, on Wednesday, 7 July 1866, at the *Olive Branch Inn* (later the *Rockingham Inn* and now *Whelan's Lion and Lobster*) in nearby Sillwood Street, Brighton. Following detailed medical and other evidence, Mr Black adjourned the proceedings for six days to allow another doctor to make a detailed analysis of the contents of the dead woman's stomach. Mrs Warder was buried later that day at the Extra Mural Cemetery in Brighton. Immediately following the service, her husband was served with a notice to attend the adjourned inquest a week later.

Following his wife's death, Alfred Warder became ill – but not through grief. The *Brighton Herald* published on the day of the inquest reported his indisposition but stated he was 'much better yesterday'. On the night of the funeral, however, the normally calm, cheerful and perfectly sane doctor appeared distraught and excited. A neighbour said that after the coroner's jury had left the doctor's house, which they had inspected, he threw up the window as if he intended to jump out. This had caused a looking-glass to fall off the wall and cut him slightly.

In fact, the evil doctor had made up his mind to kill himself directly his wife's death began to be investigated. He wrote to a friend, one Mr Elland, making arrangements for the disposal of his personal property 'in the event of anything happening' to him.

On 9 July he went to London, returning in the evening to his lodgings in Bedford Square. He decided he would go out – not far, just to the *Bedford Hotel* round the corner, taking with him what he needed. Before doing so, he asked Miss Landsell for his bill. She replied that she would make it out next day, but he insisted: 'Oh no, Miss Landsell, if it is not troubling you too much, let me have it tonight.'

She did not see him again but sent the bill up by a servant at about 8 o'clock next morning.

Leaving both his dining room and sitting room in perfect order, Dr Warder walked round to the hotel on the sea front and booked a room, saying that he had arrived in the town by the late mail train from London. The hotel staff noticed nothing peculiar about his behaviour, but when he did not appear downstairs next

The Bedford Hotel, *where Warder ended his life. It was demolished following a fire in 1964.* Chris Horlock collection

morning his room was entered and his undressed body was found lying on its left side on the bed.

Giving evidence later, Dr James H Pickford of Cavendish Place stated:

> *His eyes presented a glistening and staring appearance. This made it difficult to believe he was not alive. This peculiar appearance is typical of poisoning by prussic acid. I put my hand on his cheek and found it of marble coldness ... I looked around the room and found this bottle on a table by the bedside.*

The bottle, and a nearby glass, had contained prussic acid.

At the inquest on Alfred Warder, his brother-in-law, Richard Branwell, said he had not seen him since his sister's funeral. He had not spoken to him then because the circumstances of her death were 'so peculiar that it would have rendered it disagreeable for me to have done so.'

Miss Landsell testified that she had received a letter from her tenant, delivered by hand, which read:

> *My dear Miss Landsell,*
> *You have already suffered enough through me and mine and another death in your house would, of course, be worse. When you receive this, have the kindness to telegraph Miss Gunning, 7 Sydney Street, Brompton, London. SW, to whom you will give up what I have left at your house. I have left on the table the cash for the bills and £3 in addition, as some compensation.*
> *Believe me. Yours truly,*
> *A. W. Warder*
> *P.S. Inquire for my keys and watch.*

Replying to the coroner, Miss Landsell said the money and bills were given to her by the servant. The money settled all the bills except for the last two weeks.

His guilt, and the reason for his suicide, would not be formally established until a week later.

On Friday, 13 July, the inquest on Mrs Warder was resumed at the *Olive Branch*, where there was a large attendance of doctors After evidence had been heard it was adjourned until 16 July, when the room was again crowded with medical gentlemen.

Dr Alfred Swaine Taylor, a professor at Guy's Hospital, read out long, intricate medical reports to prove that no poisons had been found in the body, but that this was quite consistent with poisoning by aconite (also known as wolf's bane). If small doses had been given within two or three hours of death, no trace would be found in the stomach. No other man knew better than Dr Warder, he stated, how to administer aconite 'either for good or mischief.'

Dr Samuel Wilks, a lecturer at the same hospital, agreed with Dr Taylor, saying he thought the symptoms of death were mainly due to aconite poisoning.

Following the coroner's summing-up, the jury almost immediately returned a verdict that Mrs Ellen Vivian Warder had died from the effects of aconite administered wilfully and of malice aforethought by her late husband, Alfred William Warder, who had since killed himself.

The doctor's crimes, said the *Herald*, were equalled only by those of Dr Pritchard, the celebrated poisoner. There was little doubt that Dr Warder's 'self-murder,' as the paper called it, was proof that he had been responsible for his poor wife's death.

The paper suggested that Mrs Warder was not his first victim, but his third, for the doctor had been married three times, and each wife had died in suspicious circumstances.

It now appeared that his first wife, by whom he had four children still living, had dwelt apart from him for some time but died within a few weeks of their ceasing cohabitation, while his second wife, whose life he insured, survived her marriage by only eight months, dying with similar symptoms to those exhibited in the case of his third wife.

Dr Warder had lived in Ottery St Mary with his first wife, and it was there that she had died in circumstances remarkably like the last days of Ellen Warder. In that case, however, there had been no post-mortem or inquiry because Dr Warder had not reported it to the local coroner or the police and had himself signed the death certificate. He had buried her quietly and had left Ottery St Mary in search of new pastures, sending his children away.

The paper remarked:

It has not been ascertained whether an insurance had been effected on her life by her husband, but she brought him a considerable marriage portion and was married to him.

Letters from Dr Warder following the death of his third wife clearly showed his suicidal intention. A small well-worn bottle containing two opium pills indicated that he had carried poison with him for several years.

Although the police had been suspicious, they had been unable to arrest the doctor until evidence of poisoning was revealed by the coroner's court. But Brighton's police chief had arranged for the suspect to be closely watched.

After a brief consultation, the jury returned a verdict of suicide and an inventory was made of the property described by Mr Elland, all the items being declared forfeit to the Crown, in accordance with the law then prevailing in the case of suicides.

Dr Alfred Warder was buried that same night at 10.30 with no ceremony and in considerable haste. In those days suicide was regarded as a civil crime as well as a religious sin, and Christian burial was always refused. The body was conveyed to the parish cemetery in a hearse, accompanied by a few policemen holding lanterns and followed by a curious crowd attracted by the novelty of the bizarre occasion.

The coffin, covered with a black cloth, bore a brass plate inscribed 'Alfred William Warder, 1866.' After passing the chapel without stopping, it was taken from the hearse and carried quickly to the grave, which had been dug about forty yards south-east of the building on a rising part of the unconsecrated, rough ground where other suicides were buried. By the light of a couple of police lanterns, the coffin was hastily lowered into the earth. The grave was then quickly filled in. The whole ritual, from the arrival of the hearse at the gates to the completion of the interment, took about four minutes.

The bystanders slowly dispersed, talking amongst themselves. This was a night they would long remember, a night the curtain fell on one of the strangest scenes in Brighton's darker history.

CHAPTER 6

Death by Chocolate in West Street
1871

Dr Woods … was greatly struck by Edmunds' absolute indifference as to the serious position she was in.

Christiana Edmunds was a brazen liar, cunning, manipulative and totally self-absorbed. She killed without even knowing who her victim would be, as long as suspicion was diverted from herself. Her actions were the expression of an obsession, a romantic infatuation which went terribly wrong.

Her victim was a boy of only four. Sidney Albert Barker, brought down to Brighton by his parents for a holiday, paid the ultimate price for the elaborate games she was playing. The chocolate cream given to him in all innocence by his uncle, Charles David Miller of Hammersmith (also staying in Brighton) contained strychnine. The lad died a quick but agonising death.

Miller retold what happened:

I gave the little boy Sidney one of these creams … and he ate it. About ten minutes afterwards the child began to cry, and his limbs became stiff, and in about twenty minutes he died. Up to the time of his having the chocolate cream he appeared to be quite well. I ate some of the chocolates myself in the morning, and about ten minutes afterwards I felt a dizziness in my eyes and a coppery taste in my throat, and my limbs gradually became stiff, and my bones seemed 'all one.' I endeavoured to rouse myself, but was unable to do so. I became better, and sat down to dinner, when the same symptoms returned. I went to a doctor, and he saw me … My brother tasted some of the creams, and observed a peculiar coppery taste, and he spat them out. The rest of the creams were thrown away. The creams were in a bag.

A local surgeon, Richard Rugg, was called in to see the boy and found him in strong convulsions. He applied cold vinegar and water to his head and sent for a mixture while he remained with the child, but before the mixture arrived, the child died – about ten minutes after his arrival. With Mr Nicholls, house surgeon at the Sussex County Hospital, he conducted a post-mortem the following day. The body was unusually rigid, yet he was unable to discover any cause of death, other than convulsions.

On the evening of the day that his brother Charles purchased the chocolates, Ernest Miller went to Maynard's shop at 39, 40 & 41 West Street where the creams had been bought. This was only a few doors away from the home of Mrs Woodhams at No 30, where the Barker family were staying. He purchased creams of the same description, which he afterwards handed to Inspector Gibbs. These sweets were analysed by Dr Henry Letheby, Professor of Chemistry at the London Hospital, who was well acquainted with the nature of poisons. He deposed:

> *I ascertained that some of them contained strychnine, but I cannot state the exact quantity. I believe, however, that they contained altogether a quarter of a grain, which was a quantity sufficient in some cases to kill an adult. A sixteenth part of a grain is sufficient to cause the death of a child. I afterwards examined the contents of a jar that was handed to me, and I discovered a quarter of a grain of strychnine in them. The jar contained the contents of the stomach of the deceased.*

He confirmed that the symptoms displayed by the victim and his uncle were those of poisoning by strychnine.

This tragic event occurred on 12 June 1871, five years after the Warder case. At that time, Edmunds, a 43-year-old spinster (who gave out that she was 34) was lodging in Gloucester Place. She had conceived an inordinate fondness for Dr Charles Izard Beard, whose surgery was obliquely across the square at 64 Grand Parade. They had become acquainted via the doctor attending her in a professional capacity.

Nathaniel Blaker recalled Edmunds as

> *not of particularly pre-possessing appearance. She was, however, an excellent draftswoman, and had been asked by Dr Beard to copy some large anatomical drawings which it was intended should hang on the walls of the Library of the Sussex Hospital, where he was Assistant Physician.*
>
> *It is probable that at this time Miss Edmunds developed for Dr Beard one of those sudden attachments, not uncommonly seen in weak-minded and emotional people, and that this rendered her insanely jealous of Mrs Beard, whom she wished to put out of the way without attracting suspicion to herself.*

Gloucester Place at its junction with North Road. Christiana and her mother lodged in one of the houses continuing the terrace on the right. Chris Horlock collection

It was during a visit to the surgery in the summer of the previous year that Edmunds took the first step. She gave a chocolate cream to Mrs Beard, who found it tasted strange and spat it out. When he examined the sweet, Dr Beard accused Miss Edmunds of trying to poison his wife. That ended the relationship with both the Beards but it was the ending of her relationship with the doctor, which the prosecution would describe as 'a state of things scarcely consistent with the

The site of Dr Beard's house (left) is now an entrance to the University of Brighton's Centre for Contemporary Visual Arts. Nos 65 and 66 Grand Parade are centre and right. The author

relationship between a medical adviser and a female patient', which pushed the strange spinster towards the next stage of her devilish scheme. Dr Beard, while not blameless, did at least pull back from the brink of the precipice.

Edmunds' mother, Mrs A Christiana Edmunds, lived with her daughter and remembered how Christiana was 'greatly excited' after going back to Dr Beard's to obtain a retraction of his accusation. When she asked him why he had become cold towards her, he replied, understandably: 'I never respected you so much since the chocolate cream.' She was greatly excited when she came home, and walked up and down, saying, 'Oh! I shall go mad.' Her mother retorted, 'You are mad already; you, of all people, ought to be particular,' alluding to her late husband, who had died in a lunatic asylum. This was something she had never done before. Edmunds was then approaching a period in her life which she had always dreaded.

Mrs Alice Over had known Edmunds for six years and for two of those years mother and daughter had lived in her house at 16 Gloucester Place (demolished in 1933 to make way for the Astoria cinema). While there, she was ladylike, quiet, and kind in every way, an observation endorsed by a servant, Caroline Pettit, but some time before she left she was not so quiet. In about March or April 1871, she appeared very strange, and said she thought she was going mad. Her eyes were very large and dull. Mrs Over's husband, George, also remembered the woman's eyes as being full and having a wildness of expression. Her manner was excitable.

She was clearly going over the edge yet coldly and calculatingly set about shifting the blame for the chocolate cream incident in the surgery. In the words of the prosecution, she did this by pursuing 'a course of conduct so extraordinary as to be totally unparalleled in the records of any criminal court of justice.'

Edmunds' evil scheme was to begin a campaign to discredit, retrospectively, the chocolate creams sold by John G Maynard at his sweetshop in West Street. In that way, she would emerge as an innocent party and might then regain Dr Beard's affection. To lend credence to her role, she even voluntarily testified at little Sidney Barker's inquest that she and a friend had been made ill by chocolates purchased in the spring from that shop, quoting some of the symptoms of strychnine poisoning she had meantime learned. She was walking on a tightrope, however, for she was recognised by a Mrs Harriet Cole, who kept a grocer's shop in Church Street, as the last person to visit her premises before a bag of chocolate creams with 'Maynards' on it was left behind.

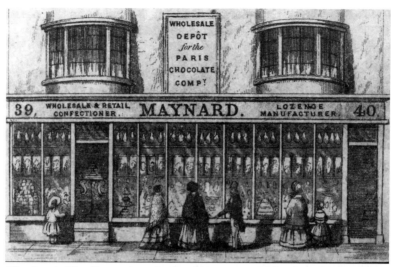

The shop in West Street where the chocolate creams which poisoned young Sidney Barker were purchased. Chris Horlock collection

However, the shopkeeper made no public mention of the fact. A Mrs Walker was given one of the sweets by her own son, Henry, who in turn had received them from Mrs Cole's daughter. She later complained to her that they had made her very ill and almost killed her.

Edmunds' first move was to purchase strychnine. Her supplier was Isaac Garrett, chemist and dentist of 10 Queens Road, to whom she claimed that she wanted to kill stray cats and, on a subsequent occasion, a dog. Garrett had dealt with Edmunds for

West Street in the 1870s, from the corner of South Street. Maynard's shop was further up on the left hand side. Chris Horlock collection

four years, selling her toiletries. Nevertheless when, on 28 March 1871, she requested a little of the poison, he objected strongly at first. She claimed the cats were destroying the seeds in her garden, and pressed him to let her have some. She said she was a married woman and had no children, and 'there was no fear of mischief' as the poison would never go out of her hands or those of her husband. Garrett ultimately supplied her with ten grains of strychnine, but required her to bring a witness. She said the only person she knew in the neighbourhood was Mrs Caroline Stone, a milliner and dressmaker (whom Garrett in fact knew well). Edmunds left the shop and fetched Mrs Stone, and upon her word Garrett made the entry of the sale in his book, which was signed first by Edmunds and then by Mrs Stone. Edmunds, he remembered, gave the name of Mrs Wood, and her address as Hill Side, Kingston, Surrey, although Edmunds told Mrs Stone that she lived in 'Kingston, near Brighton.'

When she first approached Mrs Stone, Edmunds told her she had neuralgia in the face and was going to Garrett's to purchase a remedy for it. She returned about five minutes later and then said that she wanted her to do her a great favour, which was to go and sign the book at Garrett's, in order that she might obtain some poison for stuffing birds. She said that she and her husband were naturalists.

Some time later, Edmunds told Garrett that she had used the strychnine and had thrown the paper away. On 15 April she went to his shop again, accompanied by Mrs Stone, and said that the poison had not acted, so he gave her ten grains more. She signed his book, saying the reason she wanted the poison was to kill a dog.

On 8 June, Garrett received a paper from a little boy purporting to be signed by Messrs Glaisyer and Kemp, chemists, of 11 and 12 North Street, asking him to supply them with a quarter of an ounce of strychnine. Garrett replied in a note, which he sent back via the boy. Some twenty minutes later, the boy returned with another letter enclosing half a crown, and Garrett enclosed one drachm (sixty grains) of strychnine in a bottle, labelled it and handed it with the change to the boy, who promptly completed his errand. Predictably, Thomas Glaisyer later deposed that the documents produced in court by Garrett were not in his handwriting, and he knew nothing of any application being made to him for strychnine.

The hapless Garrett was to receive another forged document on 14 July via a young messenger, Adam May, aged 11. It purported to come from the Borough Coroner, asking the chemist to send him his register of poisonous drugs sold by him.

The letter stated that the application was not in reference to anything sold by him but the book was wanted in reference to another inquiry. He gave the messenger the book, and he brought it back to him. May remembered:

The parcel contained something like a book, and I took it ... and gave it to her [Miss Edmunds], and she walked away with it. Before this we had walked together for some distance. When I gave her the parcel, she gave me fourpence-halfpenny. Not long after this I saw [her] again in King-street, Brighton, and she asked me if I should like some 'bull's-eyes.' I said I should, and she gave me some.

A few days later, Garrett noticed a leaf was missing, although it was the leaf immediately preceding the entries relating to the sale to 'Mrs Wood'. He did not see Edmunds again until she was in custody at the police-court.

Having obtained the substance she needed for her plan, Edmunds had to devise a way of getting the poison into the sweets. This she did by again using the services of willing youngsters, who would happily perform virtually any errand for a few coppers – as we have seen.

She therefore stood from time to time at various locations near Maynard's shop and got the boys to call there to buy chocolate creams for her. These she would then return for replacement, claiming she had changed her mind. But into the sweets she had randomly inserted poison.

Adam May saw Edmunds in Portland Street and was asked if he would go on an errand for her. She told him to go to Mr Maynard's shop and purchase sixpennyworth of large chocolate creams, which he did:

I saw her [the assistant] take them out of a large case, and she put them into a paper bag. I noticed that they were large ones, such as I had asked her for. The lady was waiting for me at the bottom of Portland-street, and I gave her the bag, and she undid it and looked at the chocolates and said they were not the right sort. She gave me a large piece of chocolate cream after she had untwisted the paper. This was after I had been back to the shop and told the young lady that they were not the sort I wanted. The chocolates I had taken back were put into the glass case, and I took back a sixpenny box of small chocolates. I gave these to the lady, and she said they were the right sort. She only looked at the box, and did not open it. I don't know where she got the chocolate from that she gave to me. After I had given her the box of sweets, the lady walked away, and I did not see her again until about three months afterwards ...

In court, May stated, critically: 'I am not sure that she gave me back the same bag I had given her.'

Another youngster running errands was George Brookes, who lived with his parents in Russell Street. He remembered meeting a lady in Cranbourn [sic] Street who asked him to go to Maynard's and get an ounce of chocolate creams. She gave him sixpence to pay for them. He got the creams and gave them to her, and also the change, twopence. She gave him a penny for his trouble. The lady was later positively identified as Edmunds.

Suspicions were naturally aroused at the shop, and an assistant, John Henry Parker, followed the boy Brookes, and saw him hand something to Edmunds.

William Tye, 12, lived in Brighton with his parents. In April 1871 he met Edmunds in North Street and she asked him to go to Maynard's to purchase some chocolate creams. He was to buy three ounces, and she gave him a shilling to pay for them. He got the chocolates and took them back to her. Here again, she said he had got the wrong ones and sent him back. He obtained others at the shop and gave them to her. She then went away with them, saying they were for a Mrs Field. Tye, however, believed he had taken back the same bag he had first given to Edmunds.

To lend authenticity to her ruse, even Edmunds herself went to Maynard's to complain, as was recorded at the inquest on her victim. She said she was going to have the creams tested because a lady friend of hers had eaten some chocolates bought at the shop and they had made her ill. Maynard never heard further from her as to whether she had taken this action.

In fact she did, using the services of a Mr Julius Schweitzer, analytical chemist, of 86 King's Road, Brighton. She asked him how so small a portion of chocolate cream could make her so strangely and so suddenly ill. Schweitzer treated her request very lightly, saying she was perhaps nervous and fanciful but altered his opinion when he tasted one himself. He provided a written analysis dated 23 March 1871 and she actually gave it to Dr Rugg. 'I had the analysis made entirely for my own satisfaction', she testified, 'I thought I was poisoned.' Neither she nor Schweitzer communicated their findings to Maynard, although Schweitzer, in fairness, did not know the source of the chocolates.

For his part, poor Maynard had his chocolates tested and they were found to be quite pure. He did not produce chocolates at the shop but only distributed them. At the inquest, both he and his supplier, George Ware of Marchmont Street, Russell Square, London, were exonerated from any blame. Ware felt vindicated:

My business was established in 1839 and I have made some hundred tons of this stuff and this is the first occasion on which a complaint has been made.

It was nevertheless recommended that he exercise more care when killing rats on his premises. The Coroner, unable to come to any conclusion on the case at the resumed inquest on 22 June, deduced the poison could only have come from Ware, and the jury agreed.

Maynard had the whole of his stock analysed and it was all destroyed. From July and August he carried on his business as usual.

It was in August 1871 that Edmunds, still bent on poisoning Mrs Beard and utterly indifferent to how many victims there were in the process as long as she was one of them and suspicion was diverted from herself, went to Margate. There, and afterwards in London, she devised her second extraordinary and diabolical scheme whereby, at one and the same time, a number of respectable families in Brighton (Mrs Beard's, of course, among them) received presents of cakes, sweetmeats and fruit, some of which were so crammed with arsenic as to cause the death of anyone, of whatever age, eating them.

Nathaniel Blaker remembered this episode:

One afternoon [...] , I was asked to go at once to Mr Boys, 59, Grand Parade, where I found two or three of the servants suffering from considerable collapse, pain and vomiting. I was told that this had come on after eating some fruit, peaches I think, which had just been sent anonymously. I was surprised at the severity of the attack, but thought the fruit was probably bad, and suspected nothing further. I had scarcely left this house and was on my road home, when I was asked to go to Dr Beard's house which was only a few doors from Mr Boys'. Here I found two or three of the servants suffering in exactly the same way as the servants at 59, and was told that the symptoms had come on after eating fruit of the same sort, also sent anonymously. My suspicions were now aroused, and on closer examination I found the fruit was covered with a white powder. I therefore collected all the vomited matter I could in earthen vessels which, together with the fruit, I put in a cupboard which I locked and sealed. I then communicated with the police who in the course of a day or two had collected sufficient evidence to justify them in arresting Miss Edmunds; she was committed for trial by the magistrates and lodged in Lewes Jail.

In January 1872, the *Brighton Gazette* recorded that one of Dr Beard's servants was still suffering the effects of having eaten a portion of cake sprinkled with arsenic.

It also reported the circumstances leading to the poisoner's apprehension in terms rather different from Blaker's:

> ... *she went to the Brighton police office and complained that* <u>*she*</u> *had received a parcel of poisoned fruit. This communication, coupled with her appearance at the Coroner's inquest in the preceding June, aroused the suspicions of Inspector Gibbs. Instructed by his chief, Mr White, to wait upon Mrs Beard with respect to the poisoned present received by that lady, he asked her if she was acquainted with Miss Edmunds? Mrs Beard replied she was, and then, after a pause which indicated the terrible suspicion that flashed on her mind, she disclosed to the Inspector the facts of the previous attempt to poison her by Miss Edmunds in the summer of 1870.*

Another fatal development for Edmunds was a subterfuge by Gibbs to get hold of her handwriting. Albert Barker, little Sidney's father, reported that he had received several anonymous letters after the coroner's inquest. By comparing these with the reply to a letter he himself sent Edmunds, Gibbs was able to establish that it was she who had written the letters to Barker. The game was up.

So intense was local feeling against Edmunds that her trial was transferred from Lewes to the Old Bailey. There, the prosecution's case was so powerful that the defence, completely nonplussed by the unique nature of the case, went all out for a plea of insanity. The genetic odds were admittedly stacked high in Christiana Edmunds' favour.

Her father, William Edmunds, had in his younger years been a skilled architect, designing the marine tower and other public works in Margate, where Christiana had been born.

Tragically, he developed a mental illness which was clearly suicidal and very destructive. He was always raving that he had millions of money, and in one incident attempted to knock down the medical man with a ruler, and was so violent that they had to lock him in a room. In 1843 he was received into Southall Lunatic Asylum on the authority of medical certificates. He

An engraving of Margate Harbour, 1830, showing, at the end of the stone pier, the lighthouse of 1828 designed by William Edmunds, Christiana's father. The structure survived until the Great Storm of 1 February 1953, when it collapsed into the sea after its foundations were undermined. The present concrete lighthouse was completed in 1955. Author's collection

stayed there for a year then in March 1845 entered Peckham Lunatic Asylum, where he died two years later.

Christiana's brother, Arthur Burn Edmunds, had died, in his prime, an epileptic idiot or lunatic at Earlswood Asylum for Idiots, having been an inmate for six years. Her sister suffered constantly from hysteria and in one of her fits attempted to throw herself out of a window. She died at 36 years of age.

Both her grandfathers and a female cousin were perfectly imbecile and other relations were afflicted with insanity.

When a child, Christiana had walked in her sleep and her parents had been obliged to fasten her door to keep her in her room. In 1853, she had gone to London and when she returned she was paralysed. Like her sister, she suffered from hysteria for several years and even at the time of her trial still did occasionally. The chaplain of Lewes Gaol, the Rev. J H Cole, testified that he believed her to be of unsound mind. She had been brought to the Gaol in August and was under his care until Christmas. He noted her mental condition in his journal and reported it to the governor and other persons. He noticed a very peculiar formation and movement of the eye. She had a vacant look at times. Her conversations were perfectly coherent, but they struck him as extraordinary, considering the situation in which she was placed. He found in her the most unnatural calmness and exceeding levity. When he spoke to her of her position, she broke out into a very extraordinary laugh. She seemed to have no power to fix her mind upon any grave subject and would suddenly change from tears to laughter upon frequent occasions. She did not appear to realise her position in the least.

Three medical witnesses, Dr Woods, Dr Robertson and Dr Maudsley, examined her and reported their findings.

Dr Woods, physician to the long-established St Luke's Hospital, London, had had long experience in cases of insanity. He was greatly struck by Edmunds' absolute indifference as to the serious position she was in. Her mind was so weak that she was incapable of judging between right and wrong in the same sense that other people would.

Dr Robertson, visitor in lunacy to the Court of Chancery, had a very great difficulty in coming to any conclusion as to the state of Edmunds' mind. He regarded her as bordering between criminal and insane. He too failed to impress her with the gravity of the position in which she was placed. Knowing the history of her life, he was led to regard her as morally insane, although if she administered poison for the purpose of destroying life she would know it was a wrong act intellectually.

Dr Maudsley (after whom the eminent psychiatric hospital was named) found a deficiency of moral feeling tantamount to insanity. Edmunds absolutely laughed at the idea of her life being in danger, or of anybody thinking it. The only real distress she showed was about the treatment she received in Newgate.

While Mr Serjeant Parry for the defence based his stance on Edmunds being a member of a family 'saturated with hereditary insanity', Mr Serjeant Ballantine for the prosecution declared, while not being unsympathetic about the family, that 'there was a duty that they all owed to the public' bearing in mind the woman's many acts. He knew the jury would reach an appropriate decision.

At the trial, which opened on 15 January 1872, Edmunds pleaded Not Guilty but the case against her was too strong. A hushed court heard her sentenced to death after the jury had only been out for an hour.

Nathaniel Blaker remembered the proceedings quite clearly:

> I was subpœnaed as a witness. There was nothing remarkable in the trial; it was an ordinary trial for murder. She was found guilty, but when asked, according to the usual custom, if there was any reason why sentence of death should not be passed on her, said she was pregnant. A jury of matrons was immediately ordered to be empanelled. The doors of the Court were closed, and two policemen proceeded to select the proper number of matrons from the women who were in the Court. Mr Richard Turner, Surgeon to Lewes Jail, who, of course, knew the policemen, was sitting close to me, and a few rows in front was a rather good-looking young woman; Mr Turner touched a policeman and suggested she should be selected, which was done, and she was made foreman, or forewoman, of the jury. When the proper number were chosen, they were marched up into the jury box, where they appeared with surprise and dismay depicted on their faces, and were sworn. They then retired and soon asked for the assistance of a surgeon. My name was mentioned, but I got off by representing to the Judge that I did not wish to act, having had to do with the case all through. Eventually a prison surgeon came. He wanted a stethoscope, for which a 'Bobby' was sent, who returned with a large telescope. Altogether the whole thing, except for its serious nature, was ludicrous in the extreme. After the trial Miss Edmunds was sent back to Lewes Jail. A plea of insanity had been urged at the trial for the defence, and Dr Lockhart Robertson, in his evidence, said the case was on the borderland between crime and insanity. Sir William Gull was sent down to Lewes to see her and make a report. [...] Miss Edmunds was eventually sent to Broadmoor as a criminal lunatic, where, I believe, she now is.

Christiana Edmunds, probably the subtlest and most complex of Brighton's murderers, died in that institution in 1907.

PROVOCATION, INFIDELITY AND LUST

CHAPTER 7

Survive and be Hanged
1914

*Please remember that the home and everything else is mine, and I
leave it all to my mother to bury us both.*

(Percy Clifford)

I t was a strange and short-lived marriage. The husband,
Percy Evelyn Clifford, was a half-caste, aged 32 at the
time of this case. Initially a theatrical artiste, he went on
to become an engineer. He saw military action abroad, serving with
the City of London Imperial Yeomanry for six months as a dispatch
rider in the Boer War, in the course of which he was wounded. He
was subsequently awarded a pension of 2s 6d (12^1/$_2$p) a day. After
his return, he was unable to follow any regular employment; he
drove a cab, acted as a commission agent and betted on the horses.
From 1903 until 1909 he lived in London with one Susan Hughes,
who would later testify as to his instability.

The wife was Maud Clifford (née Walton). She was particularly
attractive and first met her husband-to-be in 1909. She was then
earning her living as a prostitute and would continue to do so for
the next couple of years. On January 7 1911, the day before her
twenty-first birthday, she married Percy Clifford at St Pancras
Registry Office.

The couple then lived at various addresses in London but the
relationship was beset by problems, the main one being that Maud
still plied her trade. Clifford strongly objected and began beating
his wife. So violent did he become that she even took out a
summons against him (although he persuaded her not to proceed
with it). The couple split up in October 1912, yet it later emerged
that they met on a daily basis. Nevertheless, Maud did not reveal
her new address – a furnished flat in Brixton, not far from her
mother, who lived in Medwin Street, off Ferndale Road. Mrs
Augusta Walton would claim that the reason they had separated
was that Clifford never did any work and her daughter was forced
to sell herself on the streets in order to bring in some money.

Top: *The busy thoroughfare of North Road looking west. No 57 is lost in the distance.* Author's collection

Middle: *A very rare postcard view of North Road looking east. The Cliffords stayed in accommodation further up the hill behind the photographer.* David Shailer collection

Bottom: *No 57 North Road, Brighton, in 2004 – much as it must have looked in Percy Clifford's time.* The author

The affection which bizarrely survived between Maud and Percy would be used by him to achieve his aim. A newspaper cutting later found among his effects showed an advertisement placed in the personal column which read, 'Dimps. Do come, Belgrave, 10 Friday, Brighton, Saturday.' 'Dimps' was Maud's nickname and 'Saturday' was 4 April 1914. The trap had been sprung.

The rooms the couple took in Brighton were in the home of Tom Upton, a general porter, and his wife, Mary, at 57 North Road, not all that far from the station. They arrived about a quarter to one. Formalities were minimal, so much so that Mary Upton did not even take the couple's names. She showed them the front room on the ground floor, which Clifford accepted, remarking 'This will do. We want to stay until Tuesday.'

In the afternoon they went out, returning for tea and going out again afterwards. It was about eleven o'clock when they came back, and Maud told Mrs Upton they had been to the second house at the Hippodrome.

The next day, Sunday, they slept in until about noon and again went out in the afternoon and evening. On Monday, they were out most of the day and did not return until 11.15. Mr Upton was standing at the door as they came up the street arm-in-arm, apparently both under the influence of drink. 'The missus thought you were lost', he joked as they came indoors, to which Clifford replied 'We have had a jolly evening.'

At 8 o'clock the next morning, Mrs Upton left two teas outside their door. When she knocked, Maud Clifford called out 'All right, thank you.' For the rest of the morning, nothing was seen or heard of the Cliffords, but at about 12.30 Mary Upton heard two loud reports. She thought they were the sounds of motor tyres bursting in the street and took no further notice.

As nothing was heard of the occupants of the room by three o'clock, however, the landlady went to the door and knocked, but got no answer. She then opened the door and saw them both lying in bed. She was horrified to see blood on the man's face. Leaving the room hurriedly, she called her husband, who was down in the basement, and he rushed into the room. As he entered, he kicked against something hard. Noticing the man was lying in bed in his night attire and with blood on his face, he pulled up the blinds and saw that while the man was alive, the woman appeared to be dead.

A policeman was immediately fetched. PC Frank Miller found that what Upton had kicked against had been a revolver. It contained three live cartridges and two spent ones. On the table was a bottle which had contained whisky.

PC Miller telephoned for a doctor and police ambulance. As Maud's body was still warm, artificial respiration was attempted, but when Dr Maguire, the Brighton police surgeon, came he pronounced her dead. The victim, still in her nightwear, had died from laceration of the brain resulting from a bullet wound in her left temple and the injury could not have been self-inflicted. Singeing around the wound, and around Percy Clifford's, showed that in both cases the revolver had been fired close to the head. There was a large quantity of blood on the bedding.

Clifford was conveyed to the Royal Sussex County Hospital, where, on admission, he was seen by Mr G N Martin, second house surgeon, who thought his condition was critical. Clifford was x-rayed to locate the position of the bullet, but an operation to extract it was deemed too dangerous. The patient would not, in fact, recover until nearly ten days later.

Among items found in his clothing were two letters, one of them addressed to the Coroner of the district and the other to Mrs Clifford at 72 Isledon Road, Holloway. It was by means of these letters that the police were finally enabled to identify the pair.

On 9 April, before Mr Bush, the inquest on Maud Clifford opened at Brighton Town Hall, although little evidence was taken and the proceedings were adjourned. On Percy Clifford's discharge from hospital, he was promptly arrested and charged with murder.

At the second hearing, prosecutor Harold Pearce gave full details concerning both Maud Clifford and the couple's ill-fated marriage. Following other evidence, it was decided to send Percy Clifford to the next Lewes Assizes on a charge of wilful murder.

The trial, held on 8 July 1914, lasted only one day. The case was heard by Mr Justice Darling and the case for the Crown was presented by Mr Barrington Ward and Mr Miles Hansell, whilst Clifford was defended by Mr Stormonth Darling.

Smartly dressed in a grey suit and wearing a black tie, Percy Clifford pleaded not guilty in a clear, steady voice.

Mr Barrington Ward then opened the case, describing the crime as a cold-blooded and premeditated murder. He outlined the events leading up to the discovery of Maud shot dead in bed and of accused lying by her side, unconscious from his wound. He also read Clifford's letters, which showed that he had planned to commit the crime. In one, addressed to his mother, he had alleged that his wife was seeing three other men. He had also written:

*I am writing this as I am nearly on the verge of distraction. [...]
What I do now I do not because I am afraid but because nobody will
laugh at me and say 'I knew his wife, the way she is going on'. I
don't want to live any more, I feel quite sick.*

The letter to the Coroner was in much the same vein. Beginning,
'Sir, I am putting some work in your way', it went on to name the
three men Clifford believed his wife was seeing. In a postscript,
he wrote:

*I have tried to induce my wife to return to me and live happily, but
she says her mother has told her not to, but to be by herself. Please
remember that the home and everything else is mine, and I leave it
all to my mother to bury us both.*

Mr Martin gave evidence as to Clifford's admission and
treatment at the Royal Sussex County Hospital. He stated that a
bullet could go through certain portions of the brain and not
affect a man's mind at all. While in hospital, Clifford had said he
remembered the day he went to Brighton and the day he entered
the hospital.

The mothers of the victim and killer respectively were called.
Augusta Walton repudiated a number of statements in Clifford's
letters, and stated he professed to be very fond of his wife, but
there were quarrels, and he accused her of being unfaithful.

For her part, Mrs Ellen Clifford spoke of her son's war service.
Cross-examined, she said that after his return from South Africa
he was very excitable and eccentric and had fits. He had
threatened once or twice to throw himself from a window. His
right hand was paralysed and he had great pain in a leg. Her
daughter-in-law, she claimed, was a bad-tempered woman, who
once threw a jug of milk at her husband because he was late
coming home.

Susan Hughes, of Copenhagen Street, off Caledonian Road,
London, was an important witness. When Maud came out of
prison in 1909 after serving a short sentence for prostitution, she
went to live with Clifford and Hughes and it soon became clear
that Clifford had fallen for her. Inevitably, they later moved out
and set up home together.

Hughes recollected seeing Clifford just before Christmas,
1913. He was no longer living with Maud and was very short of
money. He seemed very depressed and said he was thinking of
finding Maud, shooting her and then killing himself. In January,
1914, Clifford called on Hughes again, this time with a revolver

in his possession. Again he said he wanted to shoot Maud and himself. Concerned for his well-being, Hughes allowed him to stay with her for a few weeks. Once he had gone, she found the revolver hidden amongst some linen but the very next day, Clifford returned and asked for it back.

Jacob Carr, a hairdresser and dealer of 28 George Street, Brighton, had known Clifford and his family for twenty years. He knew him by the nickname 'Oscar' and they were on good terms, despite him having only seen Clifford three times in the previous eleven years. When Clifford and Maud travelled down to Brighton, they met up with Carr on the Monday night – the night before Maud's death. He had a few drinks with them in a public house in East Street. He said they appeared to be on the best of terms. Clifford told him they were going back to London the next day.

The question of Clifford's responsibility for his actions was settled by the prison doctor, Dr Dow. He had had the accused under observation for some time and was of opinion that he was sane, although his mental condition was admittedly in some respects not normal.

Mr Stormonth Darling began his address to the jury on Clifford's behalf by warning them against any racial prejudice – it was, indeed, on his advice that accused had not gone into the box. The issue was whether his client was insane at the time of the tragedy. There was a great deal of evidence pointing to that, and to the fact that at various times he suffered from fits of madness or extreme eccentricity. He argued that ever since he was wounded in the war, his client's manner had entirely changed. The evidence of Susan Hughes strongly supported his (Counsel's) submission that the man was insane at times and perfectly sane at others. Just as he had been insane when he wrote the letters, he contended, so he had been insane when the tragedy occurred. On this he rested his case.

After the luncheon adjournment, Mr Justice Darling gave his summing-up. The *Sussex Daily News* reported:

> *He pointed out that the only defence set up was that prisoner was insane. What was there to satisfy them that when he killed this woman he was insane? He was sane now and, apparently, had been ever since he recovered consciousness. Prisoner shot himself, but many a man had done that when perfectly sane. Months before, prisoner had expressed his intention of killing his wife and himself and the jury had heard the letters, one of which – that addressed to the Coroner – showed that he knew exactly what would happen, and*

that there would be an inquest. What was there to show that at any time prisoner was not in his right senses? It was said he had fits, but that was a long time ago and just after he came back from the war; [...] There was no evidence that prisoner was insane for a single moment. But it was for the jury to say whether he was guilty of murder or insane when he committed the act.

It took the jury only twenty-five minutes to find Clifford guilty. In sentencing him to death, Mr Justice Darling told him he agreed that the crime was

a deliberate murder resolved on long before and perpetrated in circumstances of great treachery. At the same time you attempted to take your life, knowing it was already forfeit, no doubt. I have a duty to perform, a painful one, but I have no alternative. It is to pronounce upon you the only sentence the law allows.

He then passed the sentence of death, at the close of which accused murmured something quite inaudible before he was hurried below by the warders.

An appeal heard on 27 July before the Lord Chief Justice, Sir Rufus Daniel Isaacs, and Justices Coleridge and Avory, at which the defence asked for leave to call further medical evidence, was dismissed.

On the morning appointed for his execution, 11 August 1914, Clifford enjoyed a hearty breakfast of three eggs, two rashers of bacon and a pint of beer. Britain had been at war with Germany for a week. Doubtless for this reason, there were very few people waiting in the sunshine outside the east wall of Lewes Gaol as the prison clock struck 8.00, signalling the execution.

The hanging of Percy Evelyn Clifford was the tenth – and destined to be the last – at Lewes since the opening of the Gaol in 1853.

CHAPTER 8

The Ottoman in Warleigh Road
1938

*I got off the ottoman and tried to stop her from hitting me. I pushed
her against the table and the next I remember she was on the floor. I
have no recollection of tying the ties round her neck. I realized what
I had done and I just took it that she was dead.*

(George Badham)

At 4.15 pm on Monday, 10 October 1938, PC Wilfred
Davies, attached to New Scotland Yard, was on duty as a
telephonist and received a 999 call. A man's voice gave
him a message: 'Will you please take down this address, 43 Warleigh
Road, Brighton. There has been an accident at that address.' Asked
what he meant by 'an accident', the man replied: 'A woman is dead.'

The call was traced to a kiosk in the neighbourhood of London
Bridge Station, not far from Southwark Cathedral. PC Davies
reported the call to Brighton Police, who immediately sent
officers to the address in question. Arriving at 6.30 pm,
Detective-Sergeant Charles Ridge and his men made a shocking
discovery in the basement flat. In a 'box settee', as the *Evening
Argus* later described it, was the body of a woman, her head and
shoulders covered by a rug. From the three ligatures round her
neck, it was clear she had been strangled.

The victim was Aline Ursula Marjorie Badham, a young
mother 25 years of age. Of her infant son, there was no sign.

Some light was shed on the mystery by the resident landlady,
Mabel Elizabeth Burrell. She had that very afternoon heard
another of the arguments that had become a feature of the stormy
marriage between Mrs Badham and her husband of two years,
22-year-old George Alexander Badham.

At 1.30 Mrs Burrell had been working in the flat upstairs and
heard the young couple's raised voices downstairs. Among other
things, she heard George Badham say 'I know it. She told me so.'
and Mrs Badham replying, 'It's a lie, it's a lie.' She also heard her
husband say 'That's why you won't have anything to do with me.'
There followed the sound of two slaps and the man said, 'You
asked for that.' The baby cried. There was the sound of a scuffle.
Mrs Badham screamed twice, and then there was silence. At

Warleigh Road in traffic-free days. It was the scene of a domestic tragedy in the autumn of 1938. Author's collection

about 2 o'clock, George Badham called out 'Ta-ta' and the basement door was slammed. Ten minutes or a quarter of an hour later, Mrs Burrell went downstairs. The flat was quiet and empty.

Clearly, it was vital that George Badham be traced and questioned. A photograph and description were issued and police in Sussex and beyond were placed on full alert.

In the event, Badham literally came to them. On the day he made the anonymous call, the wretched, penniless husband spent the night at a Church Army hostel in Great Peter Street, London, giving his name as Brown. The next day, in his search for his second night's accommodation, he approached PC Ernest Broadstock, on duty in

43 Warleigh Road today. As in so many cases, the basement flat was the scene of a fatal assault. The author

Whitehall, at 10.30 pm and asked him for a ticket for a Welfare Centre. The officer provided one, followed him to the Centre and saw him enter. He spoke to a colleague, PC Dickie, who then had a conversation with Badham, from which it emerged that he had allegedly been in London for about three weeks and had been wandering about. He again gave his name as Brown and said he lived in Portsmouth. After going to Cannon Row Police Station and examining a photograph of the man, the suspicious officer returned to the Centre and interviewed him again. Badham told him he had nothing to identify himself, nor had he any luggage with him. Not satisfied with his explanation, the constable asked Badham to accompany him to Cannon Row Police Station.

There, Detective Inspector Arthur Thorp of the Metropolitan Police, attached to New Scotland Yard, interviewed Badham at 12.15 am. Still masquerading under the name of Albert Brown, the fugitive said he had no fixed address. He said his parents lived at 31 Havant Road, North End. Portsmouth, or 'they did so when I was last home.' Inspector Thorp then told him he strongly resembled a man wanted in connection with a serious offence at Brighton and asked him if there was anyone who could identify him as Albert Brown. He replied: 'No, I am all alone.'

In response to further questions, Badham reiterated his earlier story that he had been in London for three weeks. Prior to that time, he had, he claimed, worked for 18 months as an electrical assembler at Allen West's of Southampton, and previously at a cycle shop in Montague Street, Worthing.

When asked if he was quite sure his name was Albert Brown, Badham paused and replied 'Well, no. But that is as good as any other isn't it?' He declined to make a statement.

When searched, he had in his possession a halfpenny, a farthing and four foreign coins of small value. He also had a newspaper in which was a statement that Brighton Police wished to interview him.

This they wasted no time in doing. Detective-Superintendent Arthur Pelling, who had worked so tirelessly in the trunk murder cases four years earlier, had been one of the first on the scene at the basement flat. Now, in company with Detective-Sergeant Ridge, he came to Cannon Row and arrested Badham at 3.35 am on Wednesday, 12 October.

Admitting his true identity, Badham continued to maintain he had nothing to say. Pelling told him:

'We are going to take you back to Brighton, where you will probably be charged with the wilful murder of your wife.' He made no reply.

We conveyed him to Brighton at 6.17 am. I again cautioned him,
and then charged him.

Much later that morning, Badham faced the charge at Brighton
Police Court. Outside, a comparatively small crowd had
gathered. The *Brighton Gazette* reported:

Badham looked steadily and unflinchingly at the Magistrates and
did not glance round the Court as he heard the charge read over to
him. He was quite composed and was wearing a double-breasted
grey suit and a pale blue soft shirt open at the neck. His hair was
carefully groomed and brushed well back. He had a slight growth of
beard.

His parents, who lived in Southwick, called at Brighton Police
Station shortly after their son had been formally charged, but did
not attend the Police Court proceedings.

However, the father of the dead woman, Alfred Edward Gay, a
retired furrier of 44 King Street, Brighton, had a seat in court.

Pelling, the only witness, gave evidence of Badham's arrest in
the early hours of that morning. Prisoner's remand was
confirmed and his request for legal aid was granted.

Throughout the morning and during the early afternoon, a
crowd waited at the Town Hall hoping to see the suspect leave the
building. The defence team left at 4 pm and 20 minutes later,
Badham was smuggled out from a side entrance. Officers
shielded him as he walked across the pavement to a police van.
He was then driven away to Lewes, where his case would be
heard at the Assizes in early December.

For Alfred Gay, it was a nightmare week. It began with the
dreadful duty of formally identifying his dead daughter on
Monday. On Wednesday came the ordeal of the court hearing,
then on Friday the inquest on Aline was held, followed by her
funeral on Saturday. Even his landlady, a Mrs Alves, had become
involved in the case, since Badham had left his son with her at
King Street when he fled to London, telling her he was going to
look for work locally and that he would be gone no more than half
to three-quarters of an hour.

At the inquest, evidence was given that the cause of Aline
Badham's death was asphyxia due to strangulation. Dr Leonard
Robert Janes, pathologist at the Royal Sussex County Hospital,
stated that he had seen the body of Mrs Badham at her home on
the day she died, and was present the next day when Sir Bernard
Spilsbury examined it at the Mortuary.

At the detailed second hearing of the case at Brighton Police Court on Thursday, 20 October, a much clearer picture of the background to the crime emerged. Increasingly, George Badham came to be seen as a victim of provocation.

Making notes on a writing pad in the dock, the prisoner listened attentively while testimony was given that his wife had been 'spooning', to use the language of the time, with another man in a garage when he was away looking for work. It was his sister, Ivy Elliott, who had been selected by the family to reveal this bitter truth at her flat at 20 North Road on the morning of the killing. The response from her brother, who was quiet and upset on learning what had happened, was a calm one. He simply said 'That finishes it', or 'That settles it.'

Their mother was in court and, during an adjournment, collapsed. She had to be taken out, but recovered later and returned to follow the rest of the proceedings.

Under cross-examination, landlady Mrs Mabel Burrell said that as far as she could say Badham was 'ever so kind and good' to his wife. Cross-examined by Mr J B Buckwell (for Badham), she said: 'She was always the boss. She was always on at him for not earning enough money.'

It was partly to seek better-paid work and partly through marital discord that George Badham had gone to London on 21 September, leaving behind his wife and baby Alexander, aged nineteen months. On 26 September, he called on his mother in Southwick, and remained there until 1 October, when he returned home. It was alleged that he and his wife quarrelled on his return and that there were repeated quarrels after that time. It was further alleged that in some of the quarrels, Badham's wife threatened to leave home and take the child with her.

On the day of Aline's death, the couple appeared to have been on friendly terms. At 10 am, with the baby in a pram, they called on her father. She left young Alex in her husband's care while she went off to look for work. It was at about 12.15 that George Badham called on his sister and they had the serious talk that would change everybody's lives. Ivy testified:

I told him 'I have something to tell you. I don't know which way you will take it'. He said: 'What is it, is it gossip?'. I said: 'No' and that Violet, my sister, had told me. He asked if it was about Aline. I said, 'Yes,' and that on the night Aline went with Fred, my brother, to the pictures she left him after the pictures were over and she then accidentally met a young man from Edlins. They then went spooning in a garage, and she did not know whether everything was all right or not.'

When asked to explain this last phrase at the Assize hearing, Ivy Elliott replied that it referred to Aline being unfaithful to her husband.

The secret lover actually appeared as a prosecution witness at the Assizes. Henry Frederick Brownings, of Rowan Avenue, Hove, a barman, admitted there had been intimacy between himself and Aline Badham on the night of 26 September. Yet his testimony was also used to good effect by the defence, led at the trial by Norman Birkett KC.

Birkett's triumph in the Mancini case a few years earlier was unforgettable and he had lost none of his advocacy skills when he came to plead on behalf of George Badham in December 1938. It was through a combination of these skills, Badham's own sincere and genuine character, his open admission of guilt, the revelation of a startling family truth and the sympathy of the judge that the young husband came to be seen in an entirely new light.

While it could not be argued that Aline Badham had brought her death upon herself, there were certainly elements of provocation in the case. Calmly, George Badham testified as to how their differences arose:

Before we were married she had been used to dances and parties. I wasn't keen on dancing and she wanted to go alone and I objected. That started the quarrels.

George Alexander Badham, guilty of the manslaughter of his wife, Aline Ursula. Author's collection

Against his will she took a job as a barmaid, spending her wages on dance frocks. She told him she didn't want to live with him and was going to get a place of her own. When his sister told him Aline had been unfaithful, he went back to the flat to get the truth from her. He had no intention of doing her any harm. She was lying down in the bedroom and he asked her whether it was true, and eventually she said it was. She wasn't going to be without a man all her life. He walked out of the room very upset, and sat on the ottoman in the living room. His wife came in and smacked his face.

He said: 'This isn't the first time this kind of thing has happened.' and she replied. 'How dare you bring that up?' and he replied, 'You have asked for it.'

Later, when re-examined, Badham explained in subdued tones that by this he was referring to something that had happened before they were married. He married Aline Gay, he said, because she was going to have a baby, but he was not the father. He had tried to be a proper father to the boy and everyone thought he was his own child.

'Until this moment in Court when your advisers have thought it proper to have brought this matter out, have you kept it secret?' asked Mr Birkett. Badham said: 'Yes.'

His reference to the matter, he said, led his wife to punch him.

I got off the ottoman and tried to stop her from hitting me. I pushed her against the table and the next I remember she was on the floor. I have no recollection of tying the ties round her neck. I realized what I had done and I just took it that she was dead. I picked the body up and put it in the ottoman as I was afraid the landlady would come down and I didn't want her to see it.

Mr John Flowers KC, for the prosecution, asked: 'You did kill your wife, didn't you?' Badham replied. 'Yes.'

'Did you kill her because she had just admitted she had been unfaithful to you ?' – 'No, sir'.

'Why did you kill her ?' – 'She started punching me and I had to defend myself and just lost my head.'

Birkett appealed to the court in a memorable plea for compassion, pointing out that

merely because Counsel has a duty upon one side or the other, it doesn't mean, of course, that the springs of compassion fail altogether or that the wells of pity have dried up.

Mr Justice Atkinson, clearly impressed by the model prisoner, began his summing up with the words 'Acquittal altogether is impossible The choice is between guilty of murder or guilty of manslaughter.' That Badham had killed his wife by 'brutal and persistent acts of violence' there could be no doubt. The prosecution, too, had discharged their burden of proof,

> *but there was a defence in this case open to accused, not one which entitled him to a clean acquittal, but one which entitled him, if established – indeed which required the jury to find him – only guilty of manslaughter and not of murder. That defence was called defence of provocation.*

After going in some detail into the whole question of provocation, the judge portrayed George Badham as a young man whose love and affection for his family had gradually been crushed. This had led to temporary loss of reason and control. The fact that three things were tied round his wife's neck 'was the best indication of the extent to which his reason had departed.'

George Badham, a victim of love for a wayward wife and a failure to live up to her expectations, was dealt with leniently. His sentence? Twelve months' imprisonment.

CHAPTER 9

The *Blue Gardenia* Murder
1961

In this history, human weakness, desires, delights, debased
destruction and death have been made visible to you by the process
of trial

(Victor Durand QC's closing defence speech,
Lewes Assizes, 28 March 1962)

I remember Christine Holford – or Hughes, as she then was. I sometimes saw her around in Saltdean in my early teens and used to think how attractive she was. Today my house is just a few hundred yards from the bungalow where she lived with her parents.

At Christmas 1959, when she was 18, she met 31-year-old local clubowner, Harvey Holford at his club, the *Blue Gardenia*. The following July, the couple, in the face of parental opposition, eloped to Scotland. Holford had tried to win her father round ('I offered to sell my drinking clubs if it would make any difference'), but to no avail. They planned to marry in the tiny parish church of Jamestown, between Dumbarton and the southern tip of Loch Lomond, but their romantic plan was foiled by reporters tracking

them down just before the wedding and Christine's parents making her a ward of court. Within months, however, the couple obtained a High Court order which set the interdict aside. They finally married in November 1960 and in May 1961 were blessed with a daughter, whom they named Karen Lesley Tracey. It was only at the baby's christening, on their first anniversary, that Christine's parents became reconciled with the couple.

Initially they were tremendously happy, although Holford was disappointed to

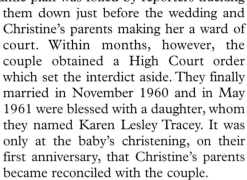

The young couple signing the register following their wedding at Dorset Gardens Methodist Church, Brighton, on 12 November 1960. The Argus

Harvey Holford with his scarlet Pontiac Parisienne, Reg. No. GYP 74, and Christine standing in his speedboat, the Christina, *in front of Barclays Bank, North Street. The car was later sold to Ben Lyons, a Hove hairdresser.* Solo Syndication

note a tendency of Christine's to flirt, first witnessed when he caught her kissing the *Blue Gardenia*'s part-time barman, Vilasar Cresteef, a Swiss student. Holford's clubs, the *Blue Gardenia* and the *Calypso* at 4 Queen Square, were well patronised. The man himself was well-off by Brighton standards and liked to flaunt the fact. His enormous scarlet Pontiac Parisienne was a familiar sight around the town's streets, often with his motor boat and trailer in tow.

In the summer of 1962, everything changed. In April, Valerie

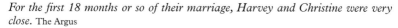

For the first 18 months or so of their marriage, Harvey and Christine were very close. The Argus

Hatcher, a 19-year-old hairdresser from Shoreham, who had become friendly with the couple, went to live as nanny to baby Karen in Queen Square. In July, she and Christine decided to have a holiday in France. Holford wanted Christine to enjoy herself and gave her £200 towards the trip.

The girls set out on the 12th from Newhaven. Christine was determined to have a good time and soon removed her wedding ring. With Valerie's knowledge, she had planned to meet up with Vilasar, who had been sacked for growing too fond of her. They joined him in Paris, where they remained for three nights. Then they went south to Cannes, with Christine paying all the fares. There, she and Vilasar shared a double room for a night at the *Hotel Albert*. Three days later they left for San Remo, where Vilasar left them for Geneva. They stayed there for about two weeks, finding it cheaper than the French Riviera. Christine soon found a new lover, a German called Fritz who was a drummer in a band. He was succeeded by an Italian restaurateur called Franco. In Juan-les-Pins, Val rejoined Christine after a trip to Nice and, on 8 August, they met Richard Reader Harris MP and he introduced them to John Bloom.

Bloom, a dazzling entrepreneur, was on the crest of a wave. He had acquired a large fortune as head of Rolls, a company which had come into being in the late 1950s after he bought the brand name of Rolls Razor to market a range of inexpensive twin-tub washing machines. During the year, Rolls amalgamated with Colston, run by Sir Charles Colston (formerly the UK director of Hoover) to market a compact dishwasher of his design. The bubble was soon to burst, however, for the joint venture went bankrupt by 1964. But that was in the future. Christine was dazzled by Bloom's wealth and possessions. He reputedly had 20 cars, three boats and a private plane. In sum, he was in a different league from far-away Holford.

Later that evening, the group went to Cap Ferrat. Here Harris had a villa, where they enjoyed drinks, swimming in the pool and, in the case of Christine and Bloom, a night of love. Harris ended up sleeping on the couch.

Christine was mesmerised by her rich lover and Bloom was doubtless already besotted with her, for he made her an astounding offer – not marriage, for he was already married – but the promise of a flat in Mayfair and another in Monte Carlo, plus £20,000 a year (although Hatcher denied this sum was mentioned). He would see her several times a week. Christine would have accepted there and then but it was not as simple as that. There was her baby daughter to consider. And, of course,

John Bloom pictured on 25 September 1969, on his way to the Old Bailey during his bankruptcy case following the collapse of his Rolls Razor washing machine business.
Hulton Archive

Harvey. Utterly naïve, she imagined her husband would have no problem with the arrangement. Would she not be in a position to buy 5 Queen Square next door as a house for him? That was something she would point out when she got back to England.

In Brighton, Holford was missing Christine greatly. He lost interest in the business, was eating badly and began drinking heavily. At the Regent Ballroom, the manager, Dennis Slade, who had managed one of Holford's clubs until September 1961, asked him what he would do if his wife did not come back to him. Holford's answer was:

> *I will probably kill her or kill myself or sell the club and get out of town.*

He also told Sheila Dunford, who helped in the club in August/September 1962, that he thought 'he might kill her.'

He did talk to Christine on the telephone from time to time but was none too pleased on one occasion to hear her ask if she could stay longer and to be told that, if she could, she would need more money. If the money had run out, he said, then it was time for her to come home. He needed the money then to pay builders.

By the morning of 11 August – his birthday – he had had enough. Taking the advice of his club manager, Peter Corvell, he rang Christine at about nine, saying he was coming over to bring her back with him. He would be in Nice that afternoon.

When he arrived, she was, he said later, like a stranger to him. Everything about her had changed – her manner, her hairstyle, her dress. Not only that, but she announced that she could never

4 Queen Square, Brighton, in September 1962. In the basement is the Whisky-a-Go Go *coffee bar, on the ground floor the* Calypso Club, *on the first floor the* Blue Gardenia Club *and on the top floor the penthouse where Christine was murdered.*
Solo Syndication

be content to live in England any more. In a walk around the quayside, she confessed to him that she had 'met this boy', later admitting that it was Bloom. She told him about the amazing offer he had made her, an offer she was about to accept, for she was on the point of moving into the Monte Carlo flat. The cash, she pointed out, would benefit them both.

They went clubbing that night in Juan-les-Pins. They both drank, but Christine got drunk while Holford stayed sober. When she pleaded that she could give him the world if he allowed her to go to Bloom, he answered 'I do not want the world, I just want you.'

The next day, the couple left Nice for a flying visit to Majorca then returned to Brighton early on 13 August. Christine had stipulated that she would return to France in two days. Harvey, desperate to take her home, agreed.

They got on tolerably well for a time and even went to Birmingham to see about opening a coffee bar. They visited her father in Saltdean and she seemed quite happy, talking of their plans to open coffee bars in university towns.

But soon the cracks appeared. Holford remembered:

When she came back she could think of nothing else but money. It was all she cared about. All she could talk about was money. She told me that she had no further interest in me and that money was all she cared about. I tried to show her the error of her ways and told her that people of her type were only interested in one thing. It made no difference. I took her out night after night, but it made no difference. All she could think about was money. That's Bloom for you, the bastard. She was a marvellous wife, that girl, until she met Bloom. It was him that did it, the bloody lot.

Terrible rows took place in the flat. Despite himself, Holford still loved Christine (he even asked a hypnotist to make him believe that he did not, as there was 'too much pain') but could not contain his fury over her behaviour. He told Corvell that he would do anything to get her back. What he dreaded was Bloom using her and ultimately casting her aside. She was too precious to him for that.

When Valerie Hatcher returned penniless to England on 18 August, she was met at Heathrow by Holford. This was not to welcome her so much as to find out the truth about what had been happening on the holiday. Hatcher confirmed that Christine had indeed slept with Bloom. He made her write an account of all that had happened, which she did in the car on the way back down to Brighton. He deposited this document with solicitors as an affidavit to use against Bloom in an enticement action, and gave Hatcher £25 for her trouble. Christine's later comment was 'That's a bloody fine friend for you.'

Holford had already found Christine's diary, which contained several names, among them that of Vilasar – and of course, Bloom. When he asked her outright if she had slept with him, she admitted she had – more than once. She was also to say that Holford's performance compared unfavourably with his. Foreigners, especially Germans, were marvellous lovers. Blind with rage, Holford gave her a savage beating. Christine said after the first blows:

I am glad you did that and showed me you are a man and not a mouse.

He later confided to Thomas Williams, an associate, friend and former proprietor of the coffee bar beneath the *Blue Gardenia*:

I hate to say this and I have probably done the wrong thing but I have cut all her hair off. I had to assert a bit of manliness over her and this will keep her indoors for at least three months.

Yet he was contrite enough to ring Mr Hughes and confess:

Christine has nearly lost her life. It isn't entirely Christine's fault. I have been unfaithful to her. I sent her to France with a girl called Valerie and she is nothing but a prostitute and a whore.

Holford later denied this was said. In any event, Hughes gave him half an hour to return his daughter to him. Holford complied.

On her return, her father found her almost unrecognisable. It looked as though there had been an attempt at strangulation. She had already been attended by a doctor in Brighton, with Holford kneeling in tears beside her. Saltdean locum Howard Sanderson noted she had severe contusions on both eyes and bruises over both cheeks and the left lower jaw. Her face was so badly swollen that he had no clear impression of the condition of her nose, but it was later found to be no longer straight.

Holford made desperate attempts to win Christine back. Taking her dancing, buying her clothes, he told her she could have a new car, anything she wanted. She was in fact given a primrose-coloured Ford Anglia on her 21st birthday on 1 September.

On that evening, they went to the *Talk of the Town* show in London, and greatly enjoyed it. On the way back to Brighton,

Christine showed Harvey a letter. She had been going to post it but after that night there was no need. He read it at an all-night coffee bar and was then deliriously happy, for it meant she would stay with him. It read:

Dear Harvey,
I'm going away from Brighton and you. Sorry, but it is impossible to forget in Queen Square. Every time I go there something inside me makes me feel very nasty towards you and I cannot go on. One thing I want in life is to have Karen and be happy, so that means I will have to work very, very hard.

We can never be happy together, and I would only end up being another Momma [Holford's mother], cleaning and working 17 hours a day. All the time I have known you, you have promised me a holiday here, there, and everywhere and the furthest I went was Brighton. It is silly to torture each other like this.

I will always keep in touch with you. I feel so lonely sitting here and am at the cross-roads. I don't know where to turn. I cannot talk to my father. I am frightened that as the years go on, once a man has hit a woman you can throw everything back into my face and do it again.
Christine

PS. Give all my love to Karen … I have never before felt in my life as I feel tonight. I wanted so much for us in the beginning. If it had not been for bad manners on both sides I feel certain we could have succeeded.

But as the days went by, the familiar pattern of rows, threats and new resolves resurfacd. The provocation continued unabated for Holford, who later told the court:

Day after day it kept building up inside of me – every bloody, stinking rotten day, she kept mentioning Bloom, Franco, Vilasar and a man called Bobby.

This was perhaps Bobby Azzan, in whose band Fritz had played.

Yet they maintained a social life of sorts, not always together. On 14 September, a Brighton Press Gang Jazz Ball, with a beauty competition judged by Frank Ifield and Janie Marden, was being held at Hove Town Hall and Holford called there to pick up tickets. Early in the evening Christine met her father for a drink in *The Plough* in Rottingdean, then visited the Warren Country Club further along the coast at Telscombe Cliffs. There she won 15 shillings at roulette. The owner's wife said 'She seemed very,

very happy and chirpy – just the same as she normally was.' She then called in for 10 or 15 minutes at the Montpelier Jazz Club in Brighton and later met her husband. He had meanwhile been very upset at the thought of her dancing, no doubt provocatively, at the Club. It seemed to be the end of the line. Dennis Slade at the Regent thought he looked terrible. Holford rang his doctor, asking about the seconal tablets he had been prescribed. Would six be enough to kill him? He was told not to be 'a damned fool.'

They went to the Jazz Ball together, after which they called in at the New Hove Albany Club. Following brief visits to the *Calypso* and the *Blue Gardenia*, they went upstairs to the flat.

Anthea Harris, a new nanny who had begun work at Queen Square on 28 August, was sitting outside the house at about midnight on the night of 14/15 September in her boyfriend's car when she saw Holford coming out of the *Whisky-a-Go-Go* coffee bar and enter the *Blue Gardenia* by the front door. Just after that, Corvell came over to her and asked her to stay out for two or three hours because Holford was having a conference up in his flat. He gave her half-a-crown to go and have some coffee, but she went instead for a drive with her boyfriend.

It was not until about 2.15 am that she returned. She noticed the lights were on up at the third floor, so remained in the car for quarter of an hour. Corvell's wife then let her in. The lights were on in the flat kitchen and there, on the draining board, she saw Christine's bloodstained wig. On going up three stairs to switch off some lights, she noticed a cardboard box with blood on it. Hesitant and fearful, she went upstairs:

I had got to within four steps of the top when I stopped because I got scared so I didn't go any farther. Then I came back down and switched the light off and went to bed. The next thing I remember is when the police came.

Holford's mother, who lived in the flat, saw the bloodied wig in the early hours as well. She alerted Corvell, who had just got home, and he returned and called the police. Detective-Constable Terry Sullivan, with two other officers, was shown upstairs by Corvell. On the kitchen table, he saw a white cardboard box and a half-pint lager glass. He saw the nanny asleep in bed and on the third tread of the stairs he found a brown, bloodstained cardboard box. Making his way to the bedroom, he found the curtains drawn.

He pulled them aside and shone his torch through the glass doors into the bedroom, directing the torch towards the bed, where he saw Holford and his wife, covered by the bedclothes and apparently asleep. Their heads were together. By the light of his torch, he could see Christine's face was bloodstained. Her mouth was slightly open and her right eye was open, fixed and staring towards the ceiling. It gave no reaction to the light. Holford lay with his arm round her, his right hand gripping her right shoulder. He was deeply asleep. Sullivan did not disturb anything and went to arrange for senior detectives, a photographer and police surgeon to come to the premises. Outside he saw Holford's Pontiac.

Unconscious from an overdose, Holford was found to be wearing only a white singlet. Christine was wearing a white pullover, black matador tights and a green blouse. From her body five bullets would be recovered. A sixth was found in the kitchen. It had gone through her jaw and was retrieved from under the stove,[3] embedded in some stale food. She had been shot three times in the head and three times in the body and lay in a pool of blood in the bed.

Holford sobbed silently in the dock at the magistrates' hearing as Sullivan told of the discovery of his wife's body. Evidence was stopped and two policemen in the dock went to his assistance when it was thought he was going to faint. When it resumed, he sat with his head bowed and his right hand shaking.

There had been a row, but this time another bombshell. Karen, she told him, was not his child.

It was a voice like a knife … I just felt something go. I snatched the gun out of the cupboard and shot her. I just shook her. I could not wake her up. I just shook her.… I just wanted to die … All I could think about was I wanted to cuddle her, that's all. It was such a strong feeling.

He had held the gun in both hands, still covered in its cloth, and did not know how many times he shot her. He had then taken tablets with water.

At 10.15 on the morning of 15 September, Sullivan revisited Queen Square and examined the bedroom, which he found to be generally untidy. There was no sign of a struggle. Looking under the bed on the side which had been occupied by Holford he found a revolver.

Not until 82 hours later did Holford recover consciousness at the Royal Sussex County Hospital. When questioned on 18 September,

---

3. According to Mr Justice Streatfeild in his summing-up, the 'refrigerator'.

he could not tell the police anything, even though he appeared rational. When Detective Superintendent Jim Marshall told him that blood traces indicated that he had carried his wife upstairs from the kitchen and put her in bed, he said he remembered nothing. His reply when told that his wife was shot six times was:

> *Completely fantastic. It is completely fantastic. It is just fantastic.*

When asked about whether he had taken an overdose of sleeping tablets, Holford replied, 'They didn't bloody work anyway.' Then when the detective asked him if he owned a revolver he answered, 'None that I know of.'

On the subject of Holford cutting off his wife's hair, the clubowner said it was standard treatment in East Germany to cut off the hair of loose women:

> *I just felt like cutting her hair. You don't know how sorry I am. A terrible thing, life, most peculiar.*

At one point during the interview, he told Marshall:

> *I will make a statement. The greatest statement you have ever heard. This will be the greatest case you have ever had.*

Following his disappointing, almost taunting, reticence with the detective superintendent, Holford was rather more forthcoming with a sergeant left with him in the hospital:

> *Briefly, my wife went to France and had it off with everyone in sight almost. I must have been insane for a while.*

Holford was remanded in Lewes Prison. There, in December 1962, he fractured his skull in a fall from the safety wire on the first-floor landing. He claimed 'I just wanted to join Christine.' In Brixton Prison, he was kept under 24-hour surveillance watch and his trial was postponed until March.

The prosecution case at his trial in Lewes was that the crime was premeditated and coolly carried out. The defence, on the other hand, pointed to the amount of seconal that Holford had taken. Only the early treatment he received had saved him from what would normally have been a fatal dose. It had been a genuine suicide attempt by a deeply distressed man.

Holford's plea was that he had not planned to kill Christine. Something snapped on the night of 15 September. Two doctors would later declare that his mental responsibility was impaired. His loss of control on the night he shot her had been precipitated by his wife's provocation.

An explanation was needed as to why he had a gun in the house. It emerged he had been fined in the past for unlicensed possession. He was, he said, interested in guns and had a collection of imitation ones. But the real one, bought from an ex-serviceman at his club, he needed for protection. He had been assaulted by three non-members, and then there were gangsters. In early May, Holford had deposited with solicitors a letter – to be opened in the event of his or his wife's death, with copies to be sent to the police and the Press Association – concerning a Legalite gaming table installed in his club. He wanted a monopoly agreement in respect of it from the leasing company, like the New Hove Albany Club had, but was told that for this he would have to put £4,000 into the firm, allegedly 'desperately short of money.' Its director then mentioned his connections, which included the notorious London gangsters Billy Hill and Albert Dimes. Holford had noted that if he did not co-operate, 'something unpleasant would happen' to him (Hill and Dimes specialised in razor slashing). Holford nevertheless made a stand. He threatened, in his capacity as a 'freelance reporter', to expose the company on television for their profiteering.

Concerning the shooting, Holford stated:

> *It is like a dream. How many times I shot her I do not know ... I just wanted to die ... I took all the tablets I could find ... I now regret doing this.*

He told the court about the improvements he made to the flat, including the penthouse he helped to build, claiming there was nothing he would not do for Christine. 'I was building a palace for my princess.'

Yet Christine had told him she did not want 'a little house or a little car' – she knew what she wanted and knew how to get it. She had called Holford 'a little boy'. The utter contempt those words conveyed was to be commented on by the judge.

On 29 March 1963, the verdict returned by the jury following the 7-day trial was manslaughter on the grounds of provocation and diminished responsibility (the applause and clapping from the public gallery was quickly suppressed).

Mr Justice Streatfeild stated:

... the jury have, I consider, perfectly rightly acquitted you of capital murder. I fully recognise there must be few men indeed who have been subjected to greater provocation than you were ... I also recognise the torturing time you must have had during the last few weeks before your wife's death.

In his summing-up, which lasted nearly three hours, the judge commented also on the fact that the names of Billy Hill and Albert Dimes had been heard by him more than once in his time as judge, among other places at the Old Bailey. The defence had already pointed out that those men bore a great responsibility for the 'adjacent position of the gun in that household.' The judge continued: 'They might not only assault him with razors but his beautiful wife too, and the thought of having her beauty slashed about with razors was too much for him.'

Harvey Leo Holford was acquitted of the murder charge and given three years for manslaughter. He was paroled on 2 October 1964.

He was again in the public eye nearly ten years later, when he – unsuccessfully – stood as independent candidate for Brighton Pavilion in the General Election under the name Robert Keith Beaumont.

The Hughes family have long been gone from Saltdean. Yet every time I pass their bungalow I think of the pretty teenager who once lived there. And of her young life cut short so suddenly and so violently in Brighton's clubland of the early 1960s.

KILLINGS OVER NOTHING

CHAPTER 10

Henry Solomon's Demise
1844

The poor fellow fell upon his hands and knees, and was utterly incapable of helping himself. He had undoubtedly at that moment received his death blow.

There must be few murders on record to which the phrase 'bolt from the blue' can so aptly be applied as the swift and brutal assault on Henry Solomon, Brighton's first Chief of Police, in his own office in the course of the routine questioning of a thief. The case is a stark reminder of the vulnerability of the guardians of the law even in the apparent security of their own premises.

Solomon was originally a watchmaker but had been in the service of the town's Commissioners since 1821. After holding various municipal positions, he was made Joint Chief Officer of Police in 1832. This, it may be remembered, was the year after that of the execution of John Holloway, and parallels will be noted between the Solomon case and that of Brighton's first trunk murderer. On the resignation of his co-equal, William Pilbeam, through ill health in 1836, Solomon was given sole responsibility as Chief Constable.

It was on the evening of Wednesday, 13 March 1844, that his path fatefully crossed that of John Lawrence (spelt in some accounts 'Lawrance'). Aged 23, Lawrence had been apprenticed in his native Tonbridge to his father as a plasterer but did not serve his time. His father died, and his mother re-married a farmer at Speldhurst. After

Henry Solomon, Brighton's first Chief Constable, met his death while on duty in a sudden, brutal attack. Author's collection

working for his stepfather for a while, he left home, drifting into a dissolute life, although he was employed for a time as a labourer on the railways. He was convicted of passing base coin and twice of a felony (during his trial, he confessed to having stolen a leg of mutton some two years earlier, to robbing his parents of £25, and other offences 'of which the public are already acquainted').

He came to Brighton about two months before Christmas 1843. Here he consorted with a gang of thieves and prostitutes, among whom he was known as 'Mag'. With them, he committed a great many petty thefts, although none of the items stolen exceeded one pound in value. He declared, however, that 'had he not been overtaken so suddenly, he should have gone on to much greater lengths.' Concerning his appearance, we know that when before the magistrates following the assault

> *he was dressed in a dark grey tweed wrapper, black silk neck cloth and had on a yellow waistcoat. He has dark piercing eyes, prominent nose, and curly hair …*

He lived in Cavendish Street (which will figure again in these pages), supported by a prostitute known as 'Hastings Bet'. But when he pawned some of her clothing, they quarrelled. So savagely did he kick and beat her that she asked for police protection. Before his attack on Henry Solomon, he had been drinking hard for several days, although he denied that he was in liquor at the time of the assault – and all the witnesses at the trial concurred.

The murderous episode at the Town Hall began with an attempted theft. On the evening in question, Lawrence and another man were seen by a woman named Catherine Hastings taking a roll of carpet from the shop door of a Mr Collins, draper, in St James's Street. One of the shop men was alerted, and Lawrence was followed up a side-street, Chapel Street, where he dropped the carpet and was taken back to the shop. The other thief escaped. At the shop, Collins handed him over to Constable John Barnden, who took him to the police offices in the Town Hall.

Solomon proceeded to examine the prisoner. Three other people were present in the room at the time: Samuel Slight, an accountant, son of the Clerk to the Commissioners; Edward Butler, the Collector of the poor-rate; and William Alger, a draper; Barnden was standing outside the door. The woman Hastings needed to be fetched for her testimony. It was while she was being sought that Lawrence carried out his assault. The

The Town Hall, where Solomon received his fatal blow, was built in 1830–32 and contained the central police station until as late as 1965. Brighton History Centre

Brighton Guardian reported the prosecution's account of the incident:

> *Solomon put one or two questions to the prisoner and prisoner in reply to one of them said he had been in the town two days, and Solomon replied that he knew he had been there a fortnight; and upon Solomon saying that, prisoner drew his stock [cravat] from his neck and said 'I am tired of my life, give me a knife, that I may make off with it.' He appeared in a state of considerable excitement. Solomon offered him no affronting language, he gave him not the slightest provocation. On the contrary, he endeavoured to compose him and told him he would not be tried there, but was merely waiting the arrival of the witness. He then turned from the spot where the prisoner stood, and the prisoner placed himself in the large chair opposite the fire. There was a gentleman in the room whom I shall call, and Mr Solomon was for a few minutes engaged in conversation with him. In the course of this conversation, the son of Mr Slight [...] was leaning on the half door; he was on one side of Solomon with his back somewhat turned to the prisoner.*
>
> *On a sudden, the prisoner rose from his chair, seized the poker, raised his hand with the poker in it and struck a blow upon the uncovered head of Solomon. It felled him to the ground. The poor fellow fell upon his hands and knees, and was utterly incapable of helping himself. He had undoubtedly at that moment received his death blow; but he was taken up by the gentlemen in the room and placed in a chair. The man at the bar made this observation, 'I know I have done it, I hope I have killed him, and I hope I shall be hung for it.' I should have told you that before Solomon was placed in the chair, the man at the bar was seized by Mr Slight, who did not see the blow struck, because it was struck by some one behind him; but he*

did see the poker descend upon the head of Solomon and immediately turned round and took the poker from the hands of the prisoner.

Solomon was carried to his home [in Princes Street, behind Pavilion Parade]; *but he was before that attended by two surgeons. He was found to have received a desperate blow on the right side of the head, of the nature of which at the moment the medical gentleman could come to no decided result. He became insensible, and I believe shortly after 10 o'clock the following morning he expired.*

There were two outstanding features of this attack. First, its ferocity. This was such as to cause a gash two and a half inches by one inch wide and the poker was bent considerably. Second, the motive, or rather complete lack of it. William Alger testified that he reproved Lawrence, saying

You wretched man (or 'you bad man'), what motive could you have against Mr Solomon?' [...] I asked him if he had any malice against Mr Solomon and he said 'none'; and I said then 'Why did you not strike me?' – for I was close by him, my elbow must have touched him – and he answered 'I did not care what I did, so that you hang me for it,' or something of that import. I could not swear to the identical word. I next asked his name, and he refused to tell me [he had given Solomon the false name of King] *and stated that he had been as respectable as any gentleman in the room and that he would not disgrace his friends by telling his name. That is all the conversation I had with the prisoner. I put several questions to Solomon. He was conscious for some time, a quarter of an hour probably; but he did not speak.*

When Solomon did speak later at his home to the surgeon, Thomas Baldey, he repeatedly expressed the concern that his assailant should not be allowed to escape and should be 'taken care of', i.e. dealt with.

The inquest on the unfortunate victim was held at 10 o'clock on Friday, the day after his death. After viewing the body, the jury returned to the Town Hall, to which Lawrence, heavily ironed and handcuffed, was brought by two policemen. He remained present throughout the inquiry, which lasted until nearly 3 o'clock.

The evidence adduced was in effect the same as that which had been given against Lawrence previously before the magistrates. The only addition of importance was the evidence of Mr Thomas Baldey giving the result of the post-mortem examination conducted that morning. He deposed that, with the assistance of three colleagues (of whom Nathaniel Blaker was one), he had examined the head of deceased and found a fracture at the lower part of the frontal bone extending in a double direction through the temporal bone into the centre of the base of the skull. There was a rupture of the meningeal artery and considerable extravasation of blood between the skull and its membranes, to the extent of about 6 ounces. Some blood was also extravasated on the opposite side of the head. These injuries were, Mr Baldey remarked, sufficient to produce death, and he had no doubt they had resulted from the blow Solomon had received on Wednesday night.

Lawrence, who appeared very dejected, declined to ask any questions and said nothing. The jury, almost without hesitation, returned a verdict of 'Wilful murder' against him and he was committed on the Coroner's warrant to take his trial at the upcoming Assizes for his crime.

At 4 o'clock, immediately after the inquest, he was conveyed to the county gaol at Lewes. On getting into the conveyance, he gave vent for the first time to his pent-up anxiety in a flood of tears.

There were many tears shed by Henry Solomon's family. Indeed, the whole town seemed to participate in an outpouring of grief.

Solomon's assailant stole a carpet from a shop in St James's Street, seen here in 1905-10. Chris Horlock collection

A vivid account of the funeral, held on the same day as the inquest, was provided by the *Brighton Guardian*:

> *Not less than ten thousand persons were present, anxious to manifest sympathy with those who had thus suddenly, and by the hands of lawless violence, been deprived of their natural protector. The whole of the Police Force with Mr Slight at its head, the High Constable, the town Beadles, and a large body of tradesmen were formed in procession, and walking in twos preceded the corpse to its last earthly home. The hearse containing the body was followed by two mourning coaches with the relatives of deceased and the Reader of the Synagogue; and all the adult members of the Congregation of Jews followed in flies* [lightweight horse-drawn carriages] *to be present and to assist at the interment. The mournful procession and the mass of people by whom it was surrounded was set in motion soon after three o'clock, and moved slowly along the Grand parade up the Ditchling road; and shortly after 4 o'clock the remains were received at the Burial Ground and after the performance of the usual service, were lowered into the grave prepared for their reception.*

A public meeting was held in Brighton on 23 March to launch a subscription for the widow and nine children of Henry Solomon. At their next meeting on 27 March the Commissioners subscribed £500. They expressed their

> *abhorrence and detestation of the cold-blooded deed which had deprived the Town of an old, faithful and valuable Servant, the country of a most zealous and vigilant Officer and a Mother and nine children of the only support on which they depended for subsistence.*

Lewes House of Correction, to which John Lawrence was initially taken. Sussex Archaeological Society Library

At the instigation of the Lord Lieutenant of Sussex, the Duke of Richmond, the Government subscribed £30 out of the Royal Bounty. The Queen contributed £50. The Jewish congregation themselves subscribed fifty guineas (£52 10s). A circus contributed the proceeds of one night's performance. The total sum received was £1,030 14s, and was invested to bring in £2 a week for Solomon's widow.

By the strangest coincidence, Lawrence saw the funeral procession. To escape observation, he was not conveyed to Lewes in a prison van, but in a barouche.[4] While on the road, he saw the crowd in the distance. 'What can all that crowd of people be about?', he asked. The policeman who was with him replied that the prisoner knew. 'It is not Mr Solomon's funeral, is it?', Lawrence enquired. The policeman replied that it was, and Lawrence coolly observed that people were very foolish to go to such sights. 'You have done the same yourself, perhaps' observed the policeman. 'No, I have not,' Lawrence replied, 'for I was in Maidstone when there were two executions and I didn't go to see either.'

He then talked on various subjects. So unconcerned was he about his victim that on going into Lewes he saw what he supposed to be a racehorse, and turned his conversation to racing, remarking that he had seen that horse run at Ascot twice.

His trial was held one week after the crime, on the second day of the Assizes (20 March) before the Lord Chief Justice, Lord Denman. Three Jewish jurors were replaced by the judge. The trial only lasted three hours, as there were three eye-witnesses of the murder and no witnesses for the defence. Counsel for the defence could only allege that the crime was committed in a momentary fit of insanity. But the Lord Chief Justice had little difficulty in showing that the circumstances did not come within the scope of the recently-formulated McNaughton rules. The jury did not retire and only took twelve minutes to arrive at a guilty verdict. The next day, Lawrence was taken from Lewes to Horsham gaol, where the death sentence was to be carried out.

It was there that a huge change came over him, just as it had 13$\frac{1}{2}$ years earlier over another notorious inmate – John Holloway. Lawrence's religious fervour was such as to merit remarks in the press.

From the time of his condemnation he had, we read, manifested a firm and pious resignation to his fate perfectly astonishing to all whose onerous duty it was to be with him, or

---

4. A four-wheeled horse-drawn carriage with a collapsible half-hood, a seat in front for the driver, and seats facing each other for passengers.

Henry Solomon's grave in the now disused Jewish Burial Ground in Florence Place, off Ditchling Road. The author

who occasionally visited him. He paid the strictest attention to the devotional exercises of the Reverend Chaplain, Mr Allen, and frequently acknowledged the great consolation he received from them. He duly rose about seven in the morning and spent the day in reading and prayer, allowing himself time only for meals (of which he partook heartily) and about an hour in each day to take air in the prison yard attended by a turnkey, with whom he would converse upon religious topics, seldom speaking upon any ordinary subject. After being visited at 8 o'clock for the last time by the Chaplain, the convict would sit up reading until he was overtaken by sleep, when he would lie down and almost invariably rest for four or five hours.

When not engaged with the chaplain, Lawrence almost incessantly occupied himself in writing and sent letters to nearly all his old abandoned associates, earnestly entreating them to renounce their present course of life and refrain from the conduct that led to his destruction.

A copy of the original painting by Henry Burstow of the county gaol at Horsham. 'X' marks the gallows. Lawrence's was the last public execution to take place there, the gaol being demolished in the following year. Chris Horlock collection

He was even granted permission to receive the Eucharist on the day before his execution (Good Friday). Indeed, he refused a visit from his brother, James, and his uncle after partaking, as he did not wish his mind to be disturbed by visits so soon afterwards. He did agree to see them early the following morning, when he made them promise they would give their hearts to God, while his brother solemnly undertook to give up all his former evil companions (this was desirable, since it was reported that his conduct during the time he had been in Horsham had 'created a universal feeling of disgust').

John Lawrence had not grown up devoid of religious instruction, and the public would learn from the press of his late father (and his mother still) being a member of the church known as the Countess of Huntingdon's Connexion. This instruction, the prisoner claimed, was now standing him in good stead.

Despite the earnest exhortations from the Rev. Mr Kendrick, the parish curate of the town's new church (described by a reporter as 'one of the most elegant edifices of the kind I ever saw in England') against any of his flock attending the execution the next day, on – of all days – Holy Saturday, a crowd estimated at between 1000 to 2000 people witnessed John Lawrence's execution. They reportedly observed the strictest order and decorum.

Praying to the last, the now-pious prisoner calmly met his end. With the words 'deliver us not into the bitter pains of eternal death' ringing in his ears, he dropped to the hereafter.

After hanging an hour, the body was cut down and removed within the prison and placed in a coffin preparatory to its interment within the precincts. Soon after dusk, the remains were deposited in the earth.

The following year, Horsham Gaol, which had been deliberately 'run down' prior to ceding its place to the Houses of Correction of Lewes and Petworth, was sold by public tender to Mr Henry Michell, brewer, of Horsham, for demolition, salvage and disposal. From William Albery, writing in 1932 in the *Sussex County Magazine* on 'The Sussex County Gaol at Horsham', comes an interesting postscript to the Solomon case:

From the land was exhumed the body of the one and last executed murderer, John Lawrence [...] This was for a short time exhibited to the morbidly curious in the 'Queen's Head' stable nearby at 2d. per head. Finally, it was transferred, the last body of a prisoner from Horsham gaol, to the south-west corner of the old churchyard, there to mingle with the dust of its unnumbered criminal, debtor, and innocent predecessors.

CHAPTER 11

A Bad Night at the *Jolly Fisherman* 1866

Three months ago it came into my mind to do this deed: to kill three; first I thought I would; and then I thought I wouldn't; and then again, I thought I would; and I came to Brighton for the express purpose of doing it.

(John W Leigh to PC Knight, 4.2.1866)

The case of John William Leigh has some close parallels with that of John Lawrence twenty-two years earlier. Both dramas were played out within a couple of hundred yards of each other in central Brighton, both the perpetrators were ruthless and unbalanced; and both victims died the following day from their injuries. Whereas in the earlier tragedy a senior officer of police was killed, in the latter another nearly lost his life – also in the course of his official duties. That surviving officer (John Barnden) was the strongest link between the cases: in 1844, when a constable, he had apprehended the criminal who would shortly kill Henry Solomon; now a superintendent, he would again take into custody a desperate character, one who had just committed murder and was quite prepared to do so again.

John William Leigh was a hard man, a heavy drinker and very violent and destructive. Not for nothing was he dubbed 'Mad Leigh' by his cronies. He was usually armed. What was worse, he was trigger-happy. It was only a matter of time before murder was added to his list of offences.

He was the illegitimate son of a Consul at Pernambuco, Brazil, his mother being a servant in his father's employment. Leigh, born in 1840, took the name of his mother, Emma Leigh, and would live with her in the Cliftonville area of Hove. She took a considerable interest in her young son, placing him in school in Ship Street, Brighton. There he received a good education. Mrs Leigh re-married and moved to London and from the age of seven until was fourteen, the lad was looked after by a lady in the town.

Yet even in his youth, he betrayed signs of that violent character which so marked his laterlife. Some old school comrades told how he showed an unusually great interest in firearms, and that one of his chief amusements was to absent himself from school to have a day's 'sport' with a pistol among the birds round Brighton. His antics around the town soon brought him to the notice of the police.

As he took a fancy to the sea, he was placed as a 'middy' on board a merchant vessel. Subsequently he entered the Royal Navy, was involved in the Crimean War taking troops out on a vessel called the *Tyrone* and took part in the hostilities in China. Whilst there he reportedly shot one of his messmates, but this was never definitively established. He jumped ship and was believed to have turned to piracy – a belief supported by the many wounds about his body. There was a reward out for his capture and he was forced to escape to England. He returned to Brighton in about 1863, and was known amongst his 'chums' as 'Captain' Leigh, on the strength of allegedly having commanded a vessel of his own. He led a wild, dissipated life for some time, and spent money in the most reckless manner.

He then became acquainted with a Miss Jane Stringer, whom he married in Lewes, having lived in St Anne's Terrace in that town for a time to be near her. Her friends were very opposed to the match. His next step was to take the *Oddfellows Arms* in Queen's Road, but he could not make it pay and left it; in 1865 he sold out £700 in the 3 per cent consols (placed there for his benefit by friends) which constituted the whole of his property.

After idling about in Brighton for some time, he moved to Brentford, Middlesex, and took a public house. When the violence of his character became known to the magistrates of the district, however, they refused to transfer the licence to him and he was compelled to give up the house. This refusal infuriated him so much he went on a rampage. He knocked out the windows, tore down the gas fittings, broke up the stairs and did much damage to the furniture. At that time, too, he was made bankrupt. For a time he evaded the police, who were after him for criminal damage, but ultimately he was compelled to give himself up. Brought before the magistrates, he was sentenced to three months' hard labour in Coldbath Fields Prison, and had only been out about two months prior to his crime in Brighton.

As might be expected, the Leighs' marriage proved a very unhappy one. He brutally ill-treated his wife, sometimes threatened to shoot her and on more than one occasion pointed a revolver at her. On his being sent to prison, his wife, left destitute, had come to Brighton to live with her sister, Mrs Harriet Harton, at the *Jolly Fisherman* public house in Market Street.

Thankfully this photograph has survived, clearly representing the Jolly Fisherman. *Here Harriet Hartan received gunshot wounds which proved fatal.* Author's collection

Market Street (south section), showing the Jolly Fisherman *set back from the road.* Author's collection

When Leigh left prison, he requested his wife several times to join him in London, but this she refused to do. On 30 January 1866, he wrote to her asking her to meet him at the *Bedford Tap* in Brighton. Notwithstanding the threat he had made against her life, and although she knew he was in the habit of carrying loaded pistols, she went along. He was reportedly seen with three pistols in his possession at that time, one of which he pointed at his wife's back. He had the idea that his sister-in-law was the cause of his wife refusing to live with him; this induced a deep animosity on his part, leading to his resolve to kill her.

The following morning he attempted to force his way into the *Jolly Fisherman* but was unable to do so. On the evening of the next day (Thursday), he met his wife, and she, surprisingly, accompanied Leigh to *Payne's Hotel*, where they shared some porter together. They only stayed a short time and on leaving must have parted, for, directly afterwards, Leigh entered the *Jolly Fisherman* – alone.

Charles Hastings, a cabinet maker, of 29 Regent Street, Brighton, recounted what happened next:

I was at the Jolly Fisherman, Market Street, last night, sitting in the bar parlour. Mr Manuel and Mrs Harton, the landlady, were also in the bar, Mr Manuel being near the door and Mrs Harton by the fire. I saw prisoner come into the bar with a revolver in his hand. As soon as Mrs Harton saw him she came to me for protection, and while she was doing so prisoner shot her, the ball going through her back and striking me on the right side of the forehead. Mrs Harton reached me and leant on my shoulder and asked me to save her. Prisoner placed the revolver within two feet of the woman's back and fired again, but I cannot say where the bullet hit her. Mrs Harton then left the bar and went down to the cellar. Mr Harton, who has kept his bed for ten months, came down stairs and tried to seize prisoner, but he escaped from him and ran out of the front door. Prisoner said nothing. All that was said was by Mrs Harton, who exclaimed, 'He's killed me; he's killed me.' I went as quickly as I could for Dr Stephens, and on my return, in about half an hour, I saw prisoner standing in the middle of Market Street with the revolver in his hand. Mrs Harton was lying on the sofa bleeding very fast. I found the bullet produced [in court] under the table in the bar parlour.

Stephen Loveday, a dyer, of 23 Pavilion Street, was outside the bar of the *Jolly Fisherman* when Leigh entered and was within a yard of him when he fired the first shot, and also saw him fire the second. Mrs Harton rushed out into the back yard and he went after her, finding her lying halfway down the cellar steps, groaning. He got her into a little room, the taproom, at the back part of the house, and seated her on a form. He remained with her till the doctor came.

Dr Joseph Stephens MRCSE, of 5 Pavilion Parade, provided medical evidence. He repaired to the scene of the crime, where he found Mrs Harton lying on a couch:

> *Some of her clothes were then taken off, and Mrs Wingfield [a neighbour] was undressing her ... I examined the woman and found a wound, apparently from a pistol shot, under the right breast; and a second wound, over the liver, about the fifth dorsal vertebra. I did not examine her closely then, because she was in a state of collapse from loss of blood. I examined her again this morning, and found that the first bullet had been right through the woman; the second had lodged in the left arm-pit and I extracted it this morning with forceps. The point of exit of the first bullet was in the lower part of the left side, between the navel and the hip bone. I produce the bullet I extracted; it has passed through the left lung. The woman is now in a state of collapse and has suffered greatly from a haemorrhage.*

Map of southern central Brighton, published 1911. It shows a number of locations mentioned in these cases. Market Street and the Town Hall may be seen at the bottom centre of the map. Brighton History Centre

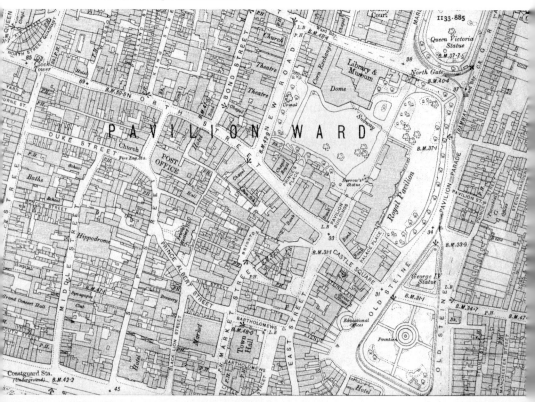

This view of the Floral Hall is a good illustration of the southern section of Market Street, now the west side of Bartholomew Square. The Jolly Fisherman *stood left, out of the picture. The Hall was demolished in 1940, as was the* Fisherman.
Author's collection

Harriet Harton succumbed to her injuries that day, directly the magistrates' hearing ended. In the midst of her suffering, she was still able to produce, or at least confirm and sign, a brief written statement describing the manner in which she was shot and the assistance given by Mr Loveday.

Leigh, it was later learned, had entered the building filled with pent-up rage. Three times before the shooting he had attempted to force his way into the house and three times Mrs Harton had shut the door against him. She was, understandably, afraid of him. The previous Tuesday evening, Mrs Wingfield, standing at her door, overhead Mrs Harton say to Leigh 'You have firearms on you, and shan't come in to my house unless you are searched.' He said, 'It's nothing to you if I choose to carry firearms about me to protect myself.' She replied 'You shan't come in unless you are searched; you're a thief, pirate and murderer.' Leigh turned round to his wife, and said 'Who told your b- sister that but you?' She said, 'I have not told her anything, Bill, so come on.' The couple then left.

Leigh's animosity had also been fuelled by events connected with a family loan. When Mr Harton was taken ill around April 1865, Leigh advanced him £50 to take the house. When Harton had to take to his bed, Leigh took proceedings against him in the County Court for the balance of the money due to him. Mrs Harton then issued a bill against Leigh for board and lodging and maintaining his wife. The balance was paid into court. Evidence was produced during the proceedings to show that nothing was any longer owed to Leigh, so money could be discounted as a motive, although it had, through Leigh's attitude, given rise to (more) ill-will.

The second crime with which Leigh was charged was the attempted murder of Superintendent John Barnden. This officer provided the following testimony:

> *Last night, just before eleven, from information I received, I went to the* Jolly Fisherman. *I saw Mrs Harton there in a fainting state, and I was told that a doctor had been sent for. I went after prisoner and found him at the King's Road end of Market street, leaning against the wall. Some one said to me, but I don't know whether it was in the prisoner's hearing, 'For God's sake don't go near him, Barnden, or he'll shoot you.' I said to prisoner, 'What's all this about?' and prisoner immediately held out a revolver to my breast and said, 'Stand off, or I'll shoot you.' I said, 'Will you, by God,' and he immediately fired the pistol. I must have touched his arm, for the ball, instead of striking me in the breast, caught the bottom of my coat and made a hole in that and my trousers. I then closed with prisoner and threw him down, and several persons came up and we brought him to the Hall. I afterwards received a coat from prisoner's wife at the* Jolly Fisherman, *and in it I found a powder flask, a cap box with caps, and thirty bullets. Mr Payne brought in a revolver, a six-barrelled one, and two of the chambers are now leaded and capped.*

Barnden's courage was fully recognised in court, where the Mayor called him into the witness-box and praised his gallantry:

> *You have most likely been the means of saving one or two lives ...* (loud cheers and continued applause in court). *I am grateful for one thing, as I'm sure we are all thankful, – that your life was preserved and that we now see you unharmed before us* (renewed cheers and applause).

At the adjourned inquest, the coroner said a document had been drawn up by the jury, which they had all signed. It read as follows:

> *The jury cannot separate without expressing their high appreciation of the courageous spirit exhibited by Superintendent Barnden under the trying circumstances of the arrest, and at the imminent risk of his life.*

Barnden's dignified bearing and humility throughout the proceedings were in stark contrast to the smiling and cynical arrogance displayed by John Leigh. He was, of course, found guilty of wilful murder. The defence's argument of insanity was dismissed but revelations of the prisoner's strange behaviour from the only two defence witnesses called were startling.

Sergeant Foy, of Brentford police, had had Leigh's public house under surveillance for four months, in view of his reputation. The man went about dressed in a strange way, and would tie and untie himself. He did not attend to his business, but shut up his house by day and filled it with ruffians at night. He would paint his face and drink hugely, yet was never seen drunk; on occasion he consumed nearly a pint of raw brandy without any serious effect. He pulled the house to pieces, breaking about a hundred panes of glass, kept a horse in the 'bar' (there being no stable) and demolished almost everything in sight. He sold off his goods, and threw away the money at the races. He occasionally suffered *delirium tremens.*

Leigh's mother, Mrs Mottley, living in London, told how her son seemed seriously disturbed when he returned from China, claiming ownership of 'a stud of horses' and 'six public houses'. She stayed with him in Brentford for a time, and saw how he lay about and usually slept in his clothes. He always carried a revolver and slept with it. He would fire it around the house, targeting various objects. He used to threaten her, not in anger, but telling her to get out of the way. He would hardly eat anything and used to take vinegar with his food and eat green unripe gooseberries, washing them down with vinegar. He used to take spirits up to his bedroom with vinegar. He would drink raw spirits, half a pint at a time – sometimes brandy, sometimes rum, sometimes taking these draughts as frequently as every half-hour, but they did not appear to intoxicate him. He was only a little more excited, not drunk. His wife was living with him while he was at Brentford, but then left, as we saw, to go to Brighton.

When Mrs Mottley visited her son in prison, she found him secured, doubtless for his own safety, and prey to the delusion that he was on board ship and in command of a vessel. He did not appear to know her. She heard he was then moved to a padded room, being so bad. On his release, his wild conduct and drinking continued as before.

Condemned to death, Leigh was contrite in Lewes Gaol. Like many in his position before and since, he turned to God. He thoroughly confessed his crime and declared his repentance. He even, for the first time in his life, received holy communion. Yet some hardness remained. He stubbornly refused to see his wife when she visited and had earlier told her that she need not come till he was swinging from the gallows!

Coldbath Fields Prison, the Middlesex House of Correction, where John William Leigh served a short sentence of hard labour. Two prisoners are seen working a crank to pump water. Rudolf Ackermann illustration from *Microcosm of London* (1808)

On Tuesday, 10 April 1866, John William Leigh paid the ultimate price for his crime.

This was an age when such an event was viewed as an entertainment for the masses. The *Brighton Guardian* covered this aspect in some detail:

> *At 11 o'clock, the rush at the Brighton Station to the Lewes train was such as sometimes may be seen prior to the departure of a special for the races, or like what has been described to take place previous to a great prize fight. The passengers, too, were of the same class, only the 'ruffianism' element was more strongly represented. So numerous and anxious were the 'excursionists' that the ordinary train was not sufficient to accommodate all, and many were compelled to wait till the second train could be got ready. No sooner had a start been made than cigars and pipes were immediately lighted, the smoking of which was continued the whole distance. Coarse, brutal and indecent jests were also freely indulged in; but the great query was 'Will Leigh die game'. On this all-absorbing point, opinion differed, but the prevailing sentiment was that he 'would stick it out like a man.'*

On the highway, which for some distance runs parallel with the railway, there were groups of pedestrians, some with their coats slung across their backs, persons in chaises and light spring carts, and others on horseback, all hurrying to the same point where the 'great event' was to come off.

The rush to get from the Lewes station was something terrific, and taxed to the utmost the patience and physical powers of two sturdy railway officials who were stationed at the gates to collect tickets. The ways from the station to the gaol were lined with passengers, all moving forward with a vigour rarely witnessed. At the spot itself there was indeed a motley crowd. The scene was striking, – strangely so, when it was considered the solemn event which was shortly to be enacted. There were the young and the old, matrons and girls, old men and lads, the younger part of the crowd greatly, however, predominating. But though the concourse was so varied, it was easily perceptible that they nearly all belonged to one class, and this class the lowest and the 'roughest' to be found in a large town. At a guess, there were between 2,000 and 3,000 persons present. For the most part they were ill and dirtily clad, but here and there could be seen an ambitious maiden who had availed herself of the occasion to display her newest spring purchases, and to make a 'holiday' of the incident.

On the whole, the crowd behaved itself well, and, though the remarks which passed between them were neither flattering nor complimentary, there was nothing of that violence and recklessness of behaviour which characterises many public executions. Vendors of nuts, gingerbread, apples and oranges were driving a flourishing trade … Mounted on chairs or aught that afforded an advantageous standing point were several individuals who were loud and demonstrative in their exhortations for the people to 'repent and be forgiven.' Wickedness in general, and Leigh's in particular, seemed the staple of their discourses … Scattered with a prodigal hand and with utter disregard to the waste of paper [were] tracts of various kinds. We should imagine, however, that the spiritual seed thus sown fell chiefly among 'thorns', and altogether the 'preaching' was anything but popular.

When the coarse ribaldry and laughter died down, the 'event' took place. It was over in a trice:

There was no struggle; and death was almost instantaneous. Such was the final scene of a life full of exciting events.… After hanging the usual time, the body was cut down and was buried on the gaol grounds close to the scaffold.

Thus was the cruel death of Harriet Harton avenged by society.

CHAPTER 12

The Violence of William Wilton
1887

The hangman, Berry, ... said that Wilton ... was the strongest-nerved man he had ever executed.

For 15-year-old George Hollingdale, the nightmare began at his home, 10 Cavendish Street, Brighton, early on the morning of 9 July 1887.

He lived there with his mother, Sarah Wilton, and stepfather, William Wilton, a wheelwright. The property had been rented since March and was so small that they all shared a bedroom. The relationship between husband and wife was a troubled one, and was not helped by them both being drinkers. Yet the evening before, a Friday, all had seemed well:

He was quite sober. Mother had prepared a nice supper of lettuce, corned beef, and onions. I had a good supper and so had mother, and father also had some. We all slept in the front room on the ground floor and went to bed a little after eleven o'clock. I was up first, at about a quarter-to-five this morning, and when I left at ten minutes past five, mother and father were in bed and perfectly quiet.

I got back at five minutes to eight. The front door was locked, and I got over the palings round the front garden and looked in at the window. Nobody seemed to be about, and after a minute or two I got in through the window. Then I saw blood dripping from the side of the bed onto the floor. I was astonished and wondered what was the cause. I could see nobody in bed. The top covering was drawn right up to the head of the bed, I pulled the covering down, and then I saw my mother with her throat cut, and blood flowing from the wound. On the washstand I saw a knife covered with blood and I immediately screamed for help and rushed for the assistance of the next door neighbour, Mr Taylor, of No. 12, Cavendish-street. Then a policeman came.

Strangely, Wilton's working clothes were found in the room so that he must have put on his best clothes before leaving the house. Young George gave the police the names of the public houses frequented by his stepfather and, surprisingly, it was only a matter of hours before the murderer was apprehended on the strength of that information alone.

The local newspaper, *The Argus*, commented:

> *The police are to be complimented upon the smart way in which they secured the arrest of Wilton. Not the slightest delay appears to have taken place in tracing the man. They ascertained that after leaving his house in the morning he had been seen to wend his way to Preston, and it was but a short while after he had visited the neighbourhood of Havelock-road that he was taken into custody at the* Windmill Inn.

This establishment was located on Dyke Road at the junction with Millers Road. Today, Highcroft Villas (previously an extension of Millers Road) stands at that junction and the *Dyke Tavern* occupies the former *Windmill Inn* site.

Wilton knew he would be tracked down. He was apprehended at 12.30 pm by PC Standing. When called outside the inn, the suspect immediately said 'I was sure you were after me when I saw you looking at the house.' The constable told him he would be charged with murdering his wife that morning by cutting her throat with a knife. He replied 'Yes, I done it; she deserved it a long time ago.' When told he would have to go to 'the Hall' (Town Hall), Wilton replied 'Yes, I will do that; I know I shall have to have the rope round my neck for her.'

When charged at the Town Hall, he responded, 'Yes, I did it.' On being searched, a razor was taken from him. It was in a case, but there were no marks of blood upon it. He also had in his pocket 2½d, a knife, and two keys, one of which he had used to lock his own house door that morning. The other belonged to the house of his brother at 53 Chester Terrace. John Wilton was an almost equally vicious character, for he made a court appearance immediately after William had been removed from the dock at his first appearance before the Magistrates. The charge was an assault on another Sarah, Sarah Knowles, who

Extract from the 1870 O.S. map showing the position of the Windmill Inn [arrowed] *on Dyke Road and its proximity to an actual mill. It stood a fair distance north-west from Cavendish Street.* Chris Horlock collection

The Windmill Inn *in around 1875, where Wilton gave himself up.* Chris Horlock collection

was seeing his son. The latter, also called John, came out of the affray with a black eye.

Following his search, William Wilton was asked to remove his clothes. He took off his coat and waistcoat, and was then asked to let down his trousers. He asked, 'What for? I own I done it.' He was wearing a flannel check shirt, the lower part of which was covered with blood, and when he saw the officers looking at the marks he said, 'That's where her head fell back; she ought to have got it long before.'

The examination of the case by magistrates at Brighton Town Hall was held very promptly – on the morning of Monday, 11 July. Public access was limited yet when the proceedings began, the courtroom was by no means overcrowded. Those who did get in, reported *The Argus*, 'supped full of horrors'.

> *Three mysterious packets were brought into court, all of them vital exhibits. The largest contained the bloodstained woollen shirt Wilton had been wearing. The second held an ordinary dinner table-knife, similar to a cheese knife, with a dull brown handle (apparently once white) and a somewhat thin blade; it was brought to view, and identified as that found on a washstand close to the bed. It was thickly stained with blood, having been used to cut the victim's throat. The third parcel contained the other weapon used in Wilton's attack, a heavy carpenter's hammer with which Sarah Wilton's skull was smashed. Both these murderous implements had been left quite openly in the family bedroom, with no attempt at concealment.*

Young George Hollingdale was called, and went bravely through his ordeal. He was followed by his neighbour, James Taylor of 12 Cavendish Street, who described the position of the corpse and the condition of the room and told how he had sent George for a policeman and went for a doctor himself.

PC George Penfold related how he had had to break the door down to get into the bedroom. He did not find the knife – it was handed to him by John Morris, the doctor.

Medical evidence was given by that practitioner, of 46 Devonshire Place (a nearby street) and Dr R P B Taaffe, of 45 Old Steine, whom we met in the Warder case and who was now Brighton's Medical Officer of Health. The victim's throat was cut from about an inch and a half under the left ear to a distance of about eight inches towards the right side. All the soft parts were divided down to the spinal column. The wound went down to the bone. It was a jagged wound as if it had been produced by the sawing of an instrument which was not very sharp. Under the circumstances it must have taken very considerable force to inflict. Morris was sure the injury could not have been self-inflicted. It would have caused death in a very few seconds.

At the time, this was the only wound apparent. On the Sunday morning, however, after the victim's body had been washed and her hair unmatted, another one an inch and a quarter long was found on the left temple, doubtless caused by the hammer produced as an exhibit. The fracture of the skull would of itself have caused death – mercifully before the cutting of the throat.

Mrs Sarah Ford, a widow, of 7 Cavendish Street, who had been an acquaintace of Sarah Wilton, had washed her body, and related how, while steadying the head of the corpse, her fingers sank into that great wound in the temple, which Dr Taaffe said penetrated to the brain and agreed could not possibly have been self-inflicted.

On the conclusion of the proceedings at the Town Hall, the prisoner was committed for trial at Lewes Assizes.

A preliminary inquest was held at 6 pm on that same day, at the *Britannia Inn*, 5 Cavendish Street. Partly because the room was not very large and partly because Wilton himself was not able to be present to hear the evidence, the proceedings were adjourned until the following afternoon at 5 pm in the Town Hall. For the moment, evidence was only taken from George Hollingdale, who confirmed he had seen the body (as had the jury) and identified it as that of his mother, aged 35. In describing the jury's visit, *The Argus* left us a valuable record of the scene of the crime and its surroundings:

> *The house where the murder was committed is situated about the centre of a small block of buildings built with boulder fronts, and No. 10 is the first of this block, having a small garden in front. The room occupied by Wilton, his wife, and the boy Hollingdale is on the ground floor and the ground giving access to it is in the passage immediately on the left of the front door. The houses are only one room thick. Wilton's room is, practically, about 11 feet square, the walls are covered with a paper of small pattern – of an ordinary bedroom pattern – and a wooden wainscot about a yard from the floor.*

This view of George Street, two streets west of Cavendish Street, gives some idea of the bustling activity in the latter in the 1880s. Author's collection

It was fairly well furnished for people in the position of Wilton and his wife, several pictures hanging on the walls, and the mantel shelf bearing a variety of ornaments, although of course not of an expensive description. The fire-place is on the left of the room, and on Saturday morning the bed was close to the wall on the west side of the room and, in fact, in the north-west corner. The washstand on which the knife was found was between the head of the bed and the door. It is a small washstand about 2 ft. 6 in. wide and is painted, grained and varnished, and has an undershelf near the floor, this being the stage on which the knife was found. Yesterday morning, the stench in the room where the unfortunate woman lay was almost unbearable, but before the time arrived for the jury to view the body, disinfecting and deodorising material had been used with beneficial effect.

When the jury arrived the bed had been drawn in the middle of the room, and the body of a woman lay in the centre, with her head to the north. All the bloodstained bedding had been removed and Mrs Wilton was covered with clean clothing. The throat was bandaged up, and the amount of linen which was required to effect the desired purpose was sufficient to give some idea of the extent of the ghastly wound beneath. The wound on the head, where it is thought the woman was struck with a hammer, was visible. The deceased appeared to be a fairly tall and well proportioned woman, with what had evidently been a pleasing countenance, and a profusion of splendid dark hair.

She had, it emerged, been an invalid suffering from an internal complaint – not specified in the press reports – for which she had been an in-patient at the Sussex County Hospital and had not long been discharged. It was said she had considerable difficulty in getting about, and when walking always gave one the impression of being in great pain. She was a peaceable woman, although she was always on at her husband. A neighbour, Mrs Rosa Bernhard, of 10 Cavendish Street (upper floors), described her as 'a very aggravating woman' and not temperate (in Jubilee week she had got in with some loafers at the house and they had spent £5 in drink over three days). When she saw Sarah on the Friday evening, the latter – ironically – appeared more cheerful than she had seen her for some time.

Sarah Wilton's funeral at the Parochial Cemetery brought together a crowd of some 200 people. It had been feared that because her friends were too poor to bury her and Wilton's relatives declined have anything to do with the matter, the parish officials would have to take the matter in hand. However, through the generosity of Mr George Denyer, undertaker, of 18/19 Lewes Road, the last painful indignity of a 'parish funeral' was averted. There was drama at the graveside when one of the deceased's friends, a Mrs Payne, went into hysterics.

The date of the County Assizes happened to fall remarkably soon after the police court hearings, namely on 10 August. During the 5-hour-long proceedings, the defence did a valiant job in attempting to show that Wilton was insane due to a hereditary taint: John Wilton, the father of the accused, swore that prisoner's grandfather on the maternal side had hanged himself, his own sister had been detained in a lunatic asylum and prisoner's brother, John, 'behaved like a lunatic'; another brother, James (deceased) had been 'strange in his head'. Mrs Elizabeth Pryor, a widow living in Hove, the sister-in-law of prisoner's father, said she remembered her father killing himself, and that she herself had been for two years and eight months in an asylum, that her sister suffered from delusions, and that the prisoner had once threatened to throw his brother over a staircase and had taken up an axe against him. Naomi Miller (prisoner's sister) said that her Aunt Harriet was peculiar in her manner. A carman named William Spicer had known Wilton since childhood and had noticed a strangeness in his manner – three years earlier he had seen him in a cowstall rolling on the floor, grinding his teeth, and his eyes 'turned in his head.' Another witness deposed that the second cousin of the prisoner's mother had died in an asylum.

The defence's theory concerning the attack was that Wilton had a struggle with his wife and in a moment of passion threw her back against the bedpost. As she was a heavy woman, the momentum was sufficient to cause the wound on the temple and kill her. The verdict therefore had to be manslaughter.

This argument was speedily demolished by the prosecution.

In his 40-minute review, Mr Justice Hawkins, stating that no mere weakness of intellect, no mere eccentricity and no mere relationship to a person who had actually been insane afforded any defence whatever, quoted from the celebrated McNaughten case for the jury's guidance. Addressing Wilton, he told him that it might be true enough, for aught he knew, that his poor wife might have given some offence in pawning some of his property, but even supposing that to be true, it was a cruel, wicked, merciless revenge he had inflicted on her without one moment's warning. He had sent her to her last account without one single moment to prepare to meet her God.

It took the jury less than quarter of an hour to bring in a verdict of Guilty.

Wilton heard the sentence unmoved. Until the week before his execution, on Monday, 29 August 1887, he showed no remorse or contrition. Only during those few last days did his father find him in a more softened mood, evidently penitent and resigned.

The scaffold was the one which had been used for Lefroy six years earlier. The hangman, Berry, who during his four years' experience had despatched as many as 106 persons, said that Wilton, whose execution was the seventh to have taken place within the walls of Lewes Gaol, was the strongest-nerved man he had ever executed.

★ ★ ★

Cavendish Street at the time of the crime was a thriving thoroughfare of 50 addresses, connecting Edward Street and St James's Street. It boasted not only an inn, but a warehouse, a lecture room and many trade premises, dwellings and lodgings. Today, little of it remains. It extends for only a few yards from the St James's Street end and contains only properties visibly numbered 2 to 5 and some waste ground. It is then straddled by Ardingly Street and the rear of blocks of flats collectively named Ardingly Court.

I doubt whether a single one of the residents or shopkeepers in this locality is aware of the dreadful crime committed here so many years ago.

Cavendish Street in the late 1930s, looking north to Edward Street, with which it connected at that time. Brighton History Centre

CHAPTER 13

A War Veteran Loses It
1943

I have done the old woman in. I have done it properly this time.
(John Dorgan to Superintendent Pelling)

I t was the summer of 1943. Brighton's townsfolk were enduring the privations of wartime life as cheerfully as possible and putting a brave face on the periodical visitations from the Luftwaffe. In May, the town had sustained its worst air attack of all when 25 raiders caused much destruction and loss of life (although four bombers were destroyed, one by a fighter and three by anti-aircraft fire). In the same month, Preston Viaduct took a direct hit: one of its arches was destroyed, dramatically leaving the rails and sleepers hanging across the gap. In another spectacular attack, two gas holders at Black Rock were bombed, setting the sky aflame with a huge orange glow.

There would be more enemy action in mid-August. During the respite, the town tried to carry on normally. Despite – or perhaps because of – the war, social activities continued unabated, with hotels, dance-halls, cinemas and public houses being much frequented.

Hotels and public houses were familiar territory to John Joseph Dorgan, a 46-year-old veteran of the First World War. He had joined up as soon as hostilities broke out in 1914 and had been awarded several medals. He had not been discharged until 1931 and had then obtained employment as a waiter and then as a potman at the *Arlington Hotel*, Marine Parade. But in July 1943 he lost his job. This meant he needed to raise money, and raise it fairly quickly. To do this he began selling possessions – mainly his wife's.

On Thursday the 29th, he was on Brighton seafront with two of his friends, George 'Bones' Windsor and Percy White. He suddenly took off his coat and sold it to a complete stranger for £1. Later the same day, in the *Queen's Head* in Steine Street, he sold a clock for 25s to Laura Emily Hobbs, an employee of the pub. That evening, he offered a camp bed to the licensee's wife, Louisa Ayling. She was naturally curious as to the reason for the sale and was told by Dorgan that there was some family trouble

Dorgan territory. The killer lived, worked and drank in streets off Marine Parade, the western end of which is seen here between the wars. Author's collection

on account of his sister's husband having left her, resulting in Dorgan needing to raise some money to pay off some debts for her. Mrs Ayling, who sensibly asked for a receipt, bought the bed and later also took a suitcase full of lady's clothing, paying £10 in total. But Dorgan pushed his luck. He later offered her even more clothes, including a fox fur. Her suspicions now aroused, Mrs Ayling not only refused the new goods but returned the items she had already bought, notwithstanding Dorgan's explanation that he was now doing 'a bit of buying and selling' for a living.

The following day, Dorgan managed to sell off some more garments at the *Queen's Head*, then returned home at 2.30 to Madeira Place, four streets away, where he shared a basement flat (8a) with his 60-year-old wife, Florence Elizabeth Agnes. This is now a guest house.

They had married in 1927. Florence had been married before and had two grown-up children from that union, but none from her unhappy marriage with Dorgan. She had for the past five and a half years been employed as a cleaner at Barclays

The Queen's Head, *Steine Street, whose sign displays a modern representation of a 'queen'. Here Dorgan sold a number of possessions of his wife's.* The author

Dorgan, his wife and their lodger occupied the basement of this guest house in Madeira Place. The author

The Aquarium *in Steine Street, another public house favoured by Dorgan. It stands at the seaward end of the street.* The author

Bank. The couple shared the property with a man named Charlie Fife, a waiter and fire watcher at the *Old Ship Hotel*. As he closed the door behind him when he left for work at 4.30 on that Friday, Fife noticed Florence Dorgan was in the kitchen, making herself a cup of tea. Her husband had already gone out about half an hour earlier, so she was alone in the flat.

Just before 7 pm, John Dorgan was seen walking along Madeira Place carrying a suitcase, with which he went into the *Aquarium Inn*.

It was only a few minutes later that Mrs Dorgan's daughter, Beatrice Primrose Blaker of 72 Hollingdean Terrace, called at the flat. There was no response to her knocking and the flat appeared to be deserted. Undeterred, Beatrice returned an hour later. Again there was no reply.

Dorgan, meanwhile, had gone from the *Aquarium Inn* to the *Queen's Head*, where he met a friend, Ernie Beazley, to whom he had the previous day offered to sell a wireless set. Dorgan offered him a pair of earrings for £7, but Ernie was still interested in the wireless, for which Dorgan wanted £9. Ernie was prepared to buy it, as long as it was in working order. Dorgan invited him back to Madeira Place to hear it for himself, together with Percy White, a furniture dealer who thought there might be a bargain or two to be had.

At the flat, Beazley heard the wireless and agreed to buy it. Dorgan said he would have it delivered to the pub the following day. During their discussions, Beatrice came back, this time accompanied by her husband, Frederick. It was now 9.20. When she looked through the basement window, she saw the three men talking. Her hammering on the front door was eventually answered by Dorgan. With feigned concern, he asked her whether she had seen her mother, who, he understood, had left earlier to walk to Beatrice's house. Beatrice, furious by this time, replied that not only had she not seen her but also that she did not believe his story. Having seen her mother the day before, she knew her stepfather had begun selling property from the flat. Even as she spoke, she saw a clock belonging to her mother was missing. Dorgan admitted to having sold it and was told in very strong terms by his stepdaughter to see he got it back.

The altercation over, the three men left the flat and went back to the *Queen's Head*. Beatrice stayed in Madeira Place, waiting to see if her mother would return. It was by then around 10 pm. Just over half an hour later, Dorgan came back. He saw Beatrice in the street talking to a neighbour, Alice Cosham, who lived next door at No 7. She had been confirming Beatrice's worst fears by telling her she had seen Dorgan earlier that day carrying out a suitcase full of goods.

Dorgan went into the flat briefly, then announced to the two women that his wife was not at home and he was going to bed. He went back in, locked the door and put out the lights. There was little else that Beatrice and her husband could do, so they went home.

Very early the next morning, Dorgan went to the *Norfolk Arms*, a public house that was allowed to open early for the benefit of users of the market. He was accompanied by two Canadian soldiers, and they had a few drinks – all paid for by Dorgan. He was joined half an hour later by Thomas Bates, a lorry driver's mate who was also a potman at the pub. Bates owned a large barrow and Dorgan arranged with him to take it to the basement flat to load up some items he had sold, including the radio to be dropped off to Beazley.

At 8.30 am, Dorgan left the *Norfolk Arms*. An hour later, Bates turned up at the flat with his barrow and the two men loaded it up. They were seen by Alice Cosham putting suitcases and the radio onto it. The barrow was then wheeled to the *Queen's Head*, where they met Beazley, who bought the wireless set and a considerable number of articles of women's clothing and small household goods which he took away in a taxi to his house in Hove.

Then the drinking continued. George Windsor turned up at the *Queen's Head* just after 10 and drank with Dorgan until 2.25 pm, with Dorgan insisting on paying for all the drinks they consumed.

Ten minutes earlier, however, Charlie Fife, who had been fire watching and working at the *Old Ship*, returned to the flat. He noticed that the room in which Florence and her husband slept was in some disorder but as it was not really any concern of his he went to his own room to get undressed. He sat on the bed and bent down to put his boots underneath. There he noticed what looked like a bundle of clothes. He reached down to pull out them out and was aghast to find that this heap was the body of Florence Dorgan. He immediately ran to the police station at the Town Hall and reported what he had seen.

Detective Constable William Lamming was first on the scene, followed by Detective-Superintendent Arthur Pelling (whom we met in the Mancini and Badham cases). The victim was eventually identified formally by her son, Sidney Ernest Pentecost, at the Royal Sussex County Hospital mortuary.

Dorgan was out visiting his favourite haunts. He met up with George Windsor again at 6.00 pm in the *Aquarium Inn*, and continued to stand him drinks. He even bought drinks for everyone in the bar. He then made his way up to Western Road, close to the Marks and Spencer store. After more drinks, he thought of making his way back to the *Aquarium Inn*. Rather than walk he ordered himself a taxi. When the car reached Steine Street, it was stopped by the police. Pelling later recalled:

> *At 8.30 pm on Saturday, 31st July I was in company with Detective Hill and Mannering in Steine-street, when a streamlined car drove round the corner from the direction of Old-stein. The accused was sitting beside the driver in the vehicle, which had to stop because of an obstruction. I opened the door and said to the accused: 'I want to speak to you, I am Superintendent Pelling.' He was conducted to a police car in waiting and when seated he said: 'I have done the old woman in. I have done it properly this time.'*

At the station Dorgan made a full written statement of his actions. He claimed that he and Florence had not been getting on well for quite some time. There were constant arguments about money (he gave her £4 a week but she was always asking for more) and because of interference from her stepchildren. This had affected his health. He had in the past suffered from malaria anyway and had been shot in the head on active service in the First World War. In fact, on July 29 1917, he had been classified as suffering from shell shock. The stress within the family only added to his problems. On the day Florence died, Dorgan had asked her to be quiet but she continued to nag him. He grabbed her by the hair and the next thing he could remember was dragging her into the front room and pushing her body under the bed.

The corpse was examined at the Royal Sussex County Hospital mortuary that same evening by the hospital pathologist, Dr L R Janes. He gave the cause of death as asphyxia due to strangulation by manual pressure and the tying of a necktie round the neck. This had been done so tightly that there was a deep depression left when it was removed. He thought she had been strangled on the settee in the middle room of the flat. Her blood group had been AB, held by only 3 per cent of the population and the same type had been found on Dorgan's trousers and shirt. Since his blood group was B, it linked him directly to the crime.

Dorgan was charged with murder at Brighton Police Court on August 2, where the presiding magistrate was the Mayor, Councillor B Dutton Briant. Only evidence of arrest was given at this stage and the case was adjourned until August 16. At the adjourned hearing, the prosecution case was that John Dorgan had coveted and desired to sell his wife's goods because he was out of work and that, in the heat of a quarrel, he had murdered her. Florence had been aware that he might try and sell her possessions for on the Friday she died, she had brought into work at the bank a Westminster Chimes clock and entrusted it to Lydia Souch, joint caretaker with William Souch.

At his last police court appearance on 31 August, Dorgan was committed for trial at the next Sussex Assizes. These opened in late November and his case was heard on 2 December before Mr Justice Charles. The accused was defended by Mr Eric Neve, who had been a member of Birkett's team defending Mancini, had taken silk in 1939 and had very recently been appointed a JP.

Dorgan had indisputably killed his wife but an attempt was made to show that he was insane at the time. He had been examined for two hours by Alexander Wilson Watt, a physician to the Lady Chichester Hospital for Nervous Disorders at Hove and to the Psychological Department of the Royal Sussex County Hospital, who had also consulted past medical reports. In his opinion, the war veteran had been unstable ever since he had been a young man, an instability aggravated by his experiences in the trenches in France. He might well have been suffering from amnesia at the time of the attack upon his wife, possibly as an after-effect of the shell-shock he had suffered all those years earlier.

The jury were not swayed by this argument. After a short deliberation, the accused was found guilty and sentenced to death. There was to be no appeal and no reprieve. On Wednesday, 22 December 1943, John Joseph Dorgan was hanged at Wandsworth by Thomas Pierrepoint, assisted by Henry Critchell.

The historic Crown Court, Lewes, where so many of the cases described in this book were heard. It is the 'Court of Drama' of Leonard Knowles' eponymous collection of Sussex murder cases (1966). The author

CHILD VICTIMS

CHAPTER 14

Frenzy in William Street
1826

Pray come to see me before I die. Farewell, farewell, farewell, my dear and precious wife.

(William Burt, writing from the condemned cell)

Shortly before Christmas 1825, readers of local newspapers would have read how a journeyman shoemaker named William Burt assaulted his young wife, Harriet. The attack took place at his mother-in-law's house, 13 Woburn Place, in the Carlton Hill district. The couple had only been married five months. They had been living in Kingston-upon-Thames since their wedding but had returned to Brighton about a fortnight before Christmas.

Harriet's mother, Ann Young, later recalled the incident:

I saw them together on the Monday week before Christmas; they were drinking tea; I neither heard nor saw anything at that time; the same evening, after I got home, in consequence of something I heard, I went back again; when I got to the door I heard someone shriek; I broke open the door, when I saw my daughter covered with blood; after this time they never lived together. My daughter lived with me until she was put to bed, which was the last day of May; the child was named Isaac. I saw William Burt the day after, he came to my door; my daughter went to Ditchling poor-house when the child was five weeks old; she returned to my house on Sunday, the 20th of August.

Harriet forgave her husband before the Sessions. Wary of his violence, however, she vowed she would never live with him again and it was for her safety that she fled to Ditchling with her infant son. By returning to Brighton, of course, she again placed herself in a vulnerable position. Burt was trying to track her down, determined that she should share his life.

On Sunday, 20 August 1826, Mrs Young unwittingly played into his hands, for she had sent for Harriet to come. She arrived at about half-past eight in the evening. Burt, however, soon picked up the scent. His mother-in-law remembered:

> *I saw William Burt between 12 and 1 o'clock, on Monday, leaning against the garden wall of my house. I asked him what he wanted. He made no reply; he went away shortly after; I have never seen him since. I told my daughter I had seen him when I went for her in the evening (she was absent that day, spending it with a neighbour) ... she trembled with fear, saying she should be injured by him.*

There was protection of a kind at Mrs Young's house in the form of William Harfield, who had lodged there for seven years. He was fond of the child and loyal to Harriet, being aware of Burt's intentions. He was in fact on first-name terms with the shoemaker but had previously resisted frequent requests – and once a 20-shilling bribe – to divulge Harriet's whereabouts. Harfield simply told him she was at Ditchling, which was then in any case true. He last saw Burt on the Monday evening, leaning on the garden wall. He said, 'Well, my man, how do you get on?', to which Burt gave an indistinct answer in a low voice.

Neither Harfield nor Ann Young could keep a constant watch for Harriet's safety, however. Both had jobs to go to. On the fateful Tuesday, Mrs Young rose at about five to get ready to leave for her work at the *Gloucester Hotel*, where she 'washed' (whether laundry or plates is not known). Harriet got up at quarter to six. Harfield took lunch with the mother and infant, but could not later say whether Burt saw them together or not. They were joined by Ann Young, on her lunch-break from the hotel.

Mrs Young went back to work at about a quarter to two, and Harfield left the house very shortly after. He had had the child in his arms during lunch and it was 'very cheerful'. When he returned at about half-past three for a shovel, he was taken aback to see a crowd at the door. At about that time, Mrs Young was summoned urgently from the hotel:

> *... a woman came to me, as I was at work, and requested me to go home immediately, as my daughter and her husband had been differing. I went home directly, and found the door locked. I heard that she was at Mrs Isted's, and went there, and found her sitting in an armchair, and covered with blood. The child was in the same room; I saw it was dying. My daughter said that her husband had killed the child. I then fainted, and was carried away.*

The dreadful crime, usually dubbed the 'Carlton Hill Murder', had not in fact taken place at Mrs Young's in Woburn Place as

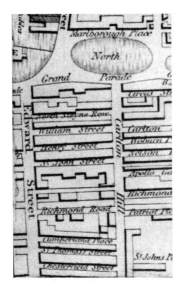

Extract from Wallis's 1830 map showing the streets between Edward Street (north side) and those on both sides of Carlton Hill.
Brighton History Centre

might be expected but in nearby William Street (five years later, the infamous Holloway trunk murder, described earlier in this volume, would be committed in Donkey Row – a stone's throw away).

Harriet and her baby had gone between ten and eleven to 32, William Street, the house of one Ann Loveridge, who had known her for the best part of a year. The young mother had already called on Ann the day before, saying that she was afraid of her husband. She called on the Tuesday to show her the child, whom she had put into short clothes. Ann Loveridge remembered that her friend 'observed how nice he looked.' At about ten past two that afternoon Harriet went back again, but this time she had obviously been shadowed. Ann Loveridge testified:

I was then at the door, when I saw William Burt behind her. I attempted to push the door to. Mrs Burt had the child in her arms. She ran up stairs. I begged him not to come into the house, saying 'Remember, Mr Burt, you almost killed your wife with a poker at Christmas, and I am afraid you will do the same if you go up stairs.'

He replied 'Where my wife goes, I will go,' and endeavoured to get by me. I put my hand on his shoulder to prevent him, and he seized me by the neck and arms and squeezed me with violence. I called to her to lock the door, which I heard her do. I said that I would fetch a beadle, which I left the house for the purpose of doing. Mr Burt was then on the third or fourth step from the bottom. I ran to Mr Taylor's on Carlton Hill, close by, to ask him for a beadle; I was not gone above two minutes, and while at his door I heard shrieks. I ran home immediately, Mr Taylor and Mr Henry Rawley following. I went up stairs first and saw Mrs Burt standing in a corner of the room, covered with blood. The face and neck of the child were also covered with blood, and it appeared to be dead. I said 'Mrs Burt, run away.' She ran downstairs and into Mrs Isted's house. I then said to him, 'Mr Burt, how could you do such a shameful thing; only think what your wife has suffered through you.'

He replied, 'Not half so much in body as I have in mind, but it is better for me to be hanged for her than that I should live such a miserable life as I do, because she will not live with me.' I then fell into hysterics, and knew nothing more.

Henry Rawley lived opposite Mrs Loveridge's house, and heard a commotion that Tuesday afternoon shortly after two. He was summoned immediately afterwards by Mr Taylor, who said that 'murder was doing.' He ran across to the house and upstairs. He met Harriet Burt on the stairs, with the child in her arms, covered in blood. He went into the room and seized William Burt, throwing him into a chair, where he held him until the officers of justice arrived. Burt several times intimated a wish to speak to him, but Taylor told him that if he had anything to say, he had better say it to the officers.

It was a sign of the times that the Coroner's jury thought nothing of visiting the injured Harriet Burt in her bedroom to get her testimony. Although weak from her wounds, she deposed as follows:

On my leaving my mother's house on Tuesday afternoon, my husband followed me to the house of Mrs Loveridge; I ran up stairs, and he burst open the door; he then took from his right-hand coat pocket a shoemaker's knife saying: 'This is for you, you d-m-n b – – h; I have had it a long time, but you shall have it now.' I cried out 'I hope you will save the child!' He then violently plunged the knife into various parts of the body of the child, and likewise into me. The blood flowed so much from my face that I could not see the child. But he continued to kick and abuse me until assistance arrived.

William Caudle, surgeon, was sent for at about half-past two. He went instantly. On arriving at Mrs Isted's house, he was shown into a room on the ground floor, where he saw Mrs Burt sitting in a chair, and in the same room was the dying infant, in Mrs Isted's lap. He was then told that William Burt had stabbed his wife and child with a knife:

On examining the child I perceived a knife, which had perforated the knee of the left leg, which knife I withdrew, and much force was necessary for that purpose. [The round wooden handle of the knife was missing, but was later retrieved and used in evidence]. *Thinking there were no other wounds on the body of the child, who was then in a dying state, I turned my attention towards the mother. At this time Mr Baldey, surgeon, arrived, and we proceeded to examine the nature of the injuries she had received.*

On such examination we perceived a wound on the right side of the neck, one on the right side of the head, another on her temples and one on the right breast, which wounds were dressed with adhesive plaster. She was then removed to her mother's house, where another wound was discovered on the right thigh, after dressing which we attended to the wounds of the infant, which was then dead.

On stripping it we discovered two wounds about an inch in length on the abdomen, through one of which wounds the intestines protruded, and which were returned into the stomach. On further examination we discovered two other wounds; one on the inside of each thigh, also a wound on the hip, on the knee, and on the breach, all which wounds appeared to have been inflicted with a knife; a great quantity of blood was issuing from the wounds, and I have no doubt but that the wounds inflicted were the cause of the death of the child.

William Baldey entirely agreed.

A subscription was opened on behalf of Harriet Burt, 'to which', pointed out the *Brighton Herald*, 'we strongly recommend the notice of the benevolent and charitable.'

The inquest was held the day after the crime at the *George the Fourth* public house and lasted from eleven till five. After being sworn, the jury proceeded to the house where the deceased infant was lying. The body was a piteous sight, with no less than seven wounds being visible on the abdomen and elsewhere. Those present were again shocked when the fatal knife, the bloody clothes of the murdered infant and three of the teeth of the

A run-down quarter of the Carlton Hill district, where Nelson Street (right) joins Sussex Street (left). Author's collection

unfortunate wife were produced. A verdict of wilful murder was returned against William Burt, and the warrant for his committal was immediately issued by the Coroner, George Gwynne.

The next morning, the prisoner was conveyed to the county gaol at Horsham until the Winter Assizes, which were to be held in Lewes in early January 1827.

In a three-hour trial, during which a death-like stillness prevailed, Burt was indicted for feloniously killing and slaying Isaac Burt and charged with assaulting Harriet, his wife. According to the *Herald*, he 'presented the most deplorable appearance'. When called on to plead, he replied, with a firm voice, 'Not Guilty.' In the course of the proceedings, he dismissed Ann Loveridge's testimony that his wife and child were in the room:

> *If you will say so in the presence of God and this congregation, you will say any thing.*

He also queried why his wife was not there to be examined, to which Judge Bayley replied that his wife could not by law be examined.

When called on for his defence, Burt produced two letters, one addressed to the judge and the other to the King; these, in accordance with his wish, were read: essentially, they were an earnest appeal for mercy, pleading the unkind and indifferent conduct of his wife towards him in extenuation of his offence; it was this conduct, he alleged, which had brought him to his present unhappy situation. During the reading of this statement, his eyes were frequently filled with tears.

These did not help him. The jury retired shortly before noon and after a few minutes' preparation returned a verdict of GUILTY.

In pronouncing sentence of death in the hushed court, Judge Bayley conceded that Burt did, in a strange way, care for his wife:

> *From the paper you have delivered you seem to have had strong feelings of regard, and, I may say, of affection towards your wife; you have, notwithstanding, committed an act which has terminated in the death of your child, and it might have terminated in the death of your wife; your wife's provocation could not possibly have excused such an act; whether you intended the death of your wife or your child, in either case the offence was great in the eyes of God, and great also in the eyes of man. Yours is the high crime of murder.*

It was ordered that he be executed the following Monday, 8 January 1827, and his body used for dissection. The judge, in passing sentence, was 'much affected' and many women were in tears. Yet Burt himself remained impassive, both when the jury returned their verdict and during the sentence and admonition of the judge.

On the following Saturday, Burt penned his last letter to his wife. It read as follows:

MY DEAR WIFE – I have now sent you my last letter that you will receive from me. I hope you are in good health and happy in your mind – as I am myself at present much happier than what any person would suppose. I seem not to fear, nor to dread death. I comfort myself by saying in mine heart I shall probably in a few hours have the pleasure of seeing my only dear little baby and your two sisters. I do not make the least doubt but that the Lord will make me amends for all my troubles and great losses which I have had in this world. I do not mean to say that I would chuse this disgraceful death rather than life, if I were to have my choice. My dear Harriet, I am very sorry that you did not come in to shake hands and bid me farewell. Let me prevail with you, my dear, to come, if possible, to see me, and let us depart without bearing malice, or having any hatred towards each other. Remember, the time will come, when you will die as well as me, and perhaps when you are on your death bed, it may be a great trouble to your mind because you did not shake hands with your poor unfortunate husband, when you had it in your power of so doing. If you can reach Horsham gaol before 12 o'clock on Monday – after that time is passed, if you would give ten thousand worlds, it would not be granted unto you. If you should come only one minute before I die, I shall be very glad to embrace the pleasure of seeing once more her whom my heart dearly loveth. I willingly, with all my heart, forgive you and your mother, likewise all other persons who have in any way tried to persuade you to never have made up matters – to be reconciled – and to have lived with me again. Pray come to see me before I die.

Farewell, farewell, farewell,
My dear and precious wife,
WILLIAM BURT

She did go. She left Brighton on Monday morning, and reached Horsham at half-past eleven. She was immediately admitted into his cell and they had a short interview, during which he begged her forgiveness, which she readily granted. While in the condemned cell, Harriet Burt appeared paralysed with terror at the awful preparation with which she was surrounded.

Having taken leave of his wife, the murderer was escorted to the chapel, where he received the Sacrament. After this, preceded by the chaplain, the Reverend Wetherby, reading the burial service, he walked with a firm step to the place of execution. On arriving at the fatal drop, he walked to the front and calmly surveyed the crowd. After about a minute, he addressed them as follows in rather tremulous voice:

My friends, I hope you will all take warning by my fate. You see before you an unfortunate man, who is just going to die. I acknowledge the justice of my sentence. Let me beg of you to watch over your tempers and passions, and resist all provocations, – (here he stopped, then continued in a choking voice) *if possible, – and I hope the Lord will have mercy on my soul.*

The executioner came forward, conducted him to the centre of the drop and adjusted the noose round his neck. The chaplain then read a portion of the 51st Psalm, and repeated the Lord's Prayer. At the end of it, at precisely 22 minutes past 12, the drop fell and William Burt departed this world.

Nearly a thousand people witnessed the execution, a great number of whom were females. These, observed the *Herald*, were 'chiefly of the lowest class.'

Seeing the characterless walls which look down on William Street today (ironically belonging for much of their length to the law courts and police headquarters), it is difficult to visualise there were once dwellings, teeming with life, on either side of that thoroughfare. One of its long-departed abodes, however, will always be assured of its place in Brighton's history of infamy.

William Street in the 1930s. It was here that the 'Carlton Hill' infanticide took place.
Brighton History Centre

CHAPTER 15

The Epileptic Delivery Man
1891

The Birmingham Daily Mail, *commenting on the Brighton murder, says it 'is one of the most revolting and brutal that has come to light for some time. It is one of those crimes upon children which are the disgrace of the century.'*

(*The Argus,* 14 December 1891)

n 1988, a fascinating book entitled *Back Street Brighton* was published. It was a compilation of photographs and memories of Brighton in the Thirties, and formed a sequel to *Backyard Brighton* – which had, incidentally, featured William Street.

Of special interest in the present case are the recollections in the former volume by one Louisa Tincknell of her home in Kemp Town:

I lived in Bedford Buildings for the first eighteen years of my life. We moved out in 1932 and our house was demolished. It had been a happy little house and we had a very pretty garden; we often had people walk by to admire the gardens. Large blocks of flats have been built on the site since.

They were very nice little double-fronted, country-style, large cottages; two up, two down. There were only nineteen houses in the street: eight on the north side, plus the stable yard that had belonged to the Stag Inn *when it was a coach house, and 11 on the south side. They were spaced well apart; one side facing to the pavement, the other side each facing the other with gardens between.*

On Friday, 11 December 1891, The Argus also left us a description:

Bedford-buildings opens off Upper Bedford-street, about half way up on the right hand side. You enter it by an arch of masonry, over which the name of the place is displayed. There is only a paved footway running through it, some of the houses having walled gardens to them. The front door of No. 8 opens right on the footpath, the house having no garden.

The sad reason for the reporter's visit was that, through one of the vilest crimes in Brighton's history, tragedy had descended on No 8, occupied by the Jeal family.

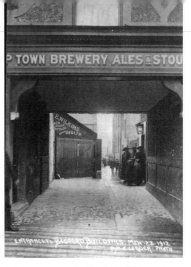

Bedford Buildings looking west, 22 March 1912, showing the alleyway access to the properties and the walls around their gardens. Chris Horlock collection

The access to Bedford Buildings through the Stag Inn, March 1912. Chris Horlock collection

A frenzied assault the previous night, committed not far away, had taken 5-year-old Edith away from them. An elder sister, whose married name was Cook, had come over from her nearby home at 4 Montague Street to comfort her parents and the rest of the large family. Because of the terrible events of the last twenty-four hours, Mrs Jeal was utterly grief-stricken and had been unconscious the whole afternoon through hysterical fits. Edward Jeal, her husband, had had no sleep the night before, having been out with a police constable searching for Edith. He worked as a milk carrier for the St James's Dairy (where one of the sons also assisted with the work of the business) and had gone straight on to work that morning without even the chance to change his clothes.

Bedford Buildings looking east, with the gardens displaying an unkempt appearance. Chris Horlock collection

Edith had been next in age to the youngest, a little boy of two-and-half. Another brother, Bertram, had accompanied her on her last errand. He was a bright, intelligent lad of nine but was too young to understand what had happened to his little sister. In fact he seemed 'quite merry' to the visiting reporter, who added 'It is as well that it is so.'

What had happened?

Bertie explained:

At about 8 o'clock I was sent by my father on an errand. My sister Edith Jeal went with me. We bought a bundle of wood and some chestnuts and then went to Trengrove's at the corner of Manchester Row. I went into the shop leaving my sister outside. She had a bundle of wood and the chestnuts in my cap. I was about three minutes in the shop and when I came out she was gone.

Edith had got the wood from Clark's fish shop, a few doors away from their home. Trengrove's the grocer's, stood on the east side of Upper Bedford Street, 60 or 70 yards away from where they lived.

When the boy got home, his mother asked him where his sister was. He replied that he did not know. He supposed she had gone home without him. Mrs Jeal was not unduly worried at first, imagining that Edith had fallen in with some of her school companions and was playing in the street. After a while, her husband went in search of the child for about half-an-hour and then at 9 o'clock anxiously went to report the disappearance at Freshfield Road Police Station (a stone's throw away from Bedford Buildings). Both parents and their neighbours scoured the neighbourhood – in vain. The night was bitterly cold, yet the child's mother, though not at all a strong woman, stayed out searching for hours.

At noon the following day, little Edith's body was found, horribly mutilated. It lay in a large barn-like storage shed located behind houses in a field between Eastern Road and Chesham Road, Kemp Town.

A PLAN OF THE SPOT.
The following is a sketch plan of the scene of the murder.

The cross indicates the spot where the body was found.

From The Argus *of 12 December 1891. Sketches of any kind were extremely rare in newspapers at that time.* The Argus

The discovery was made quite accidentally by Corporation workman Edward Villiers, who was working on trees in nearby Rock Street. He alerted his mate, William Stanford, who chanced to see the carriage of a local surgeon, Mr Frederick Humphry, not far off. The doctor later recalled:

> *On Friday December 11th I was in Chesham-road about 12.45. I found a man talking to my coachman and at his request I accompanied him to a shed in a field behind the houses on the north side of Chesham-road. The entrance to the shed is on the east side. On entering the shed I saw the child lying dead, its head near to the east wall on the north side of the door. I looked at the child and examined it superficially. The body was lying with the feet towards the south-west, the left leg drawn up and the right leg extended. The child was on its back. The lower part of the body was bare, the clothes being thrown up on to the chest. I noticed the hair was matted with blood, the face very much swollen, livid, bruised and scratched. I looked at the neck because the child looked as if it had been strangled. I looked for a ligature round the neck but found none. The lower part of the body was very much injured, bruised and lacerated. I turned the body over and found the left thigh was bruised and scratched, and a quantity of blood underneath on the ground, and not on which the child lay. The child's clothes were smothered with blood. The child's drawers were lying about yard from the body of the child on the left-hand side between the body and the door. They were saturated with blood. The child's straw hat was lying very near the head. The floor of the building was covered with mould or some loose dry earth. I am of the opinion that the child died from asphyxia. I should say the child had been dead between 12 and 18 hours when I saw it. Rigor mortis had set in both in the legs and arms. The shed was so dark I could not make a minute examination.*

The Argus recorded on Saturday, 12 December:

> *A crime of unspeakable atrocity was brought to light in Brighton yesterday – a crime even more indescribably horrible in its circumstances than any of the Whitechapel murders. In the case of the murders in East End of London almost the whole of the facts could be made public; but in the case of this lawless and terrible revelation of lust in the East End of Brighton there are facts so horrible that they can never be placed before the general public in the columns of a newspaper.*

Elsewhere in that issue, the writer imagined the lonely scene of the murder the night before:

Where the poor child was left in her blood, the rain could be blown in upon her so long as it continued; but the rain ceased in the early hours of the morning, and the silent stars and the white moonlight shone down on that dark shed in which a crime of such unutterable horror had been committed.

The day that paper appeared, the inquest on the body of the child was opened at 5 o'clock at Freshfield Road Police Station by the Deputy Borough Coroner, A Freeman Gell. The jury having been sworn, they proceeded to view the body which was lying in the mortuary attached to the station. The remains of the little one lay out on a large slab in the centre of the building covered by a blanket. The uncovered corpse was a sad sight. The child's dark brown hair lay carelessly over her pretty face and her throat bore marks of terrible violence. Most of the bruises were on the right side of the face and extended from the forehead to the mouth.

Edward Jeal was the first witness and had the painful duty of formally identifying the body as that of his daughter. He also detailed the circumstances of the child and her brother being sent out to make purchases.

PC Herbert Pelling also testified, while detailed medical evidence was provided by Dr Douglas M Ross. Of the many injuries the child had received, he believed only one was inflicted after death, indicated by a discoloration of the abdomen and apparently caused by a blunt instrument. She had (to use the language of the time) been violated. In later testimony, he revealed that on the external organs of generation he had found a severe laceration extending from the upper part, while Mr Humphry would testify at the trial that 'The lower part of the body was much injured, especially the private parts.'

The inquest was adjourned until Saturday, 19 December, when the whole case was considered in greater detail.

Yet even on the morning the initial inquest was held, a suspect had faced the charge of wilful murder at Brighton Police Court. His name was George Henry Wood. He was 29 years of age and lived with his father at 11 Rock Street, the eastward continuation of Chesham Road. His home was only a couple of hundred yards from the field.

For the last eighteen months he had been employed as a van man in the Goods Department at Brighton Railway Station, which involved making deliveries of parcels and other consignments to various addresses. On account of a number of connected, suspicious sightings and actions at the time of the murder and after it, he had attracted the attention of the police.

It was particularly unfortunate for Wood that one witness was

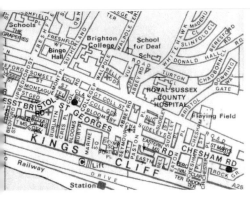

Contemporary map showing part of the Kemp Town area. Upper Bedford Street and Freshfield Road both abut Eastern Road on the left side of the map.
Estate Publications/Ordnance Survey

View of St Mary's Hall School, Eastern Road, from the South Field where Edith Jeal met her end. The St Mary's Place development now covers the site.
Chris Horlock collection

Chesham Road looking west. The field stood behind the houses on the right, and the barn/shed in the vicinity of the back garden walls of the row of low-roofed dwellings.
Author's collection

Extract from the 1898 1:2500 map showing relevant locations. The structure shown in the South Field ['rectangular' feature between Chichester Place and Chesham Road] is intriguing, but the barn/shed had long been demolished by this date.
Brighton History Centre

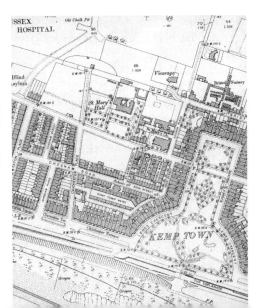

actually a constable, PC Tuppen, who had first met him ten years earlier and could positively identify him as the man seen in a drunken state on the night of the crime.

Wood was taken into custody by Detective Inspector Samuel Jupp at 8 o'clock in the evening of the day the body was discovered. When apprehended, he declared he had been at the Circus in North Road on Thursday night, yet could produce no corroborating witness. An identity parade was held in the large room at the back of the Police Court, to which several children who had been accosted were taken and asked if they could point out from the twelve men gathered there the one who had spoken to them. In almost every instance the children singled out Wood.

At the Brighton police court hearing on 12 December, Wood was charged with wilfully murdering Edith Jeal. Evidence was heard from Edward Villiers, William Stanford, Edward Jeal, PC Pelling and Detective Inspector Jupp.

Edward Jeal spoke about the events of the terrible night and how, at 1.40 the following afternoon, his son had come and told him he was wanted at Freshfield Road Police Station. There he saw the body of his child.

PC Herbert Pelling told how he had been on duty at midday the day before in Sussex Square and had been approached by Edward Villiers, whom he accompanied to the field. This was used for football and cricket by the boys of nearby Arlington House School, under a lease agreement with St Mary's Hall School, Eastern Road. There he saw Edith Jeal's body, whose life was pronounced extinct by the doctor. From Freshfield Road Police Station, Pelling then ordered an ambulance, into which he placed the body, Bertram's cloth peaked cap found at the crime scene, the firewood and Edith's drawers.

Detective Inspector Jupp reported going to the Goods Department at Brighton Station at around eight and asking Wood whether he had been in Lavender Street at about 8 o'clock the night before. He said he had not. He even claimed not to know PC Tuppen.

He was asked to accompany Jupp to the Police Office at the Town Hall, which he did 'very solemnly and quietly.' On being charged with outraging and murdering Edith Jeal, he very faintly replied, 'No, sir.' When put into the cells, he appeared somewhat dazed. Asked if he understood the charge, Wood said 'Yes, but I don't remember one particle about it.'

He was ordered to undress. Considerable marks of blood staining were found on his trouser flap, which was very damp as if it had been partially washed, and on the outside of his cord trousers. These were blue and dirty. Bloodstains were also found on his flannel under-shirt and cotton over-shirt, with indications of washing. A slight blood mark was found on his woollen drawers. On 14 December, the Chief Constable, James Terry, forwarded the clothes worn by Wood on the night of the murder to Guy's Hospital for analysis by Dr Stevenson, the Home Office analyst. A thorough search of Wood's house was also carried out.

The Winter Assizes were due to be held the following Wednesday, but there was no way the case would be ready by then. Despite the defence's protests, the prisoner would simply have to be detained for some months. Meanwhile, Wood was to make two more appearances at Brighton Police Court.

What do we know of this reprehensible character and his family? Some of the facts are surprising.

The eldest of eight children, his appearance was, according to *The Argus*, such that:

James Terry was Chief Constable of Brighton from 1881 to 1894. He joined the force in 1843 and on retirement had served for over 50 years. The townspeople raised a subscription for him totalling £600 and purchased Hoathly Villa in Florence Road, Preston, for him.
ESRO, Ref. SPA 10/5/6

> ... *one would suppose him to be physically a somewhat strong man; with his florid complexion, fair moustache, blue-grey eyes, and rather frank and straightforward expression of countenance, he is far from being an ill-looking man.*

Yet the reporter at his trial described him as:

> ... *somewhat under medium height, with an extraordinarily weak, characterless face, low forehead, flat cranium, his head appearing curiously small in proportion to his rather broad shoulders. His appearance suggests a certain physical smartness but very little intelligence.*

As a child he had been frail. He had his first epileptic fit at the age of two (his epilepsy would acquire some importance during later proceedings). When he was three, he fell ill. The doctor, according to Mr Wood Snr, said 'they would never rear him', on account of the compression on the brain he was suffering from. He was emaciated and vague during childhood but got better when he was eight or nine. He had several jobs as an errand boy and later went to sea but was discharged on account of malformation of the chest and scabies contracted on the ship. After that he tried working on a farm close to Brighton and then went into the country. This was followed by seven years in Canada. On his return, he took up his current employment with the local railway company and conducted himself well (although a record of some instances of petty theft in Brighton would later emerge).

He was now engaged, to a young lady who 'bears a high character'. The couple were originally to have been married during the week beginning 14 December, but the wedding had been postponed until the following Easter.

The only real insight we have into his mind after the murder was left to us in the form of a letter written a few days afterwards to his parents. It was as near to a written confession as one might hope for. It was read out by a court official both at the adjourned magistrates' hearing on 22 December (during which Wood once or twice burst into tears) and at his trial the following spring, when he again cried. Extracts are reproduced here in all their repetitiveness, illiteracy and inconsistency:

From your Loving Loving son George.
My dear Father and Loving Mother and my dear darling Lizie. It is with deep sympathy and the love of God which I feel deep depths of my Heart this morning that I write to you this morning, this is all through breaking the pledge which you all thought I was keeping …

I had never broken the pledge till last thursday week since I joined it. I drive the horses alright on thursday without any accident whatever. I remember driving in the station gates alright on thursday night but I do not remember anything more after I got inside of the gates. I can't remember anything that happened after was through the Beastly drink. I must have been helplessly drunk. I am very sorry very sorry to have to say such a thing. It as fairly broke me up. I prayed to the Lord Jesus this morning and he as give me courage to write you this morning this crime as been brought to my feet but as God is my keeper and my helper I do honestly say that I do not remember or cant bring my bring myself to remember anything whatever about it or can I bring myself to believe it was done by your son George I don't know I am sure what my Dear Love Lizie will think of me after two long years of courtship and to think that we were going to be married at Easter …

My poor Lizzie I don't know what will become of her if anything should happen to me tell her not to cease writing to you for I am sure this will drive her to her sister's in Canada but if I am not to see her no more tell her she must come down to see me …

It would not be so bad if I knew what I had done but I have not the least recollection of anything occurring after tea time on Thursday.

This as nearly drove me out of my mind last night I thought it was my last for I saw the golden city and the gates open ...

I needed your advice scores of times but I never heeded it God grant that this may make us all Love the lord Jesus Christ more and more than we have ever done before ... I needed him last week but I need him more but this morning I found a true friend in him ...

Look after Lizie don't go back on her keep her from going abroad if possible I should like to see her very much indeed it would cheer me up greatly if I could and now I must say good bye and God bless you and may his face shine upon you and may he always be near you when help is most needed give my kind love to all and kiss them all for me and especially to Dar Lizie give my kind love to her and kiss her for me God grant that she may always walk the path of Ritchousness for his name sake Amen and ask her to pray for me and remain your ever Dear Son George

Wood's parents were people of the highest respectability and irreproachable character. For nearly a quarter of a century his father had occupied a prominent position at Belgrave Street Congregational Church and was one of its Elders at the time of his son's arrest. Sunday after Sunday, for many years, he might be seen conducting strangers to vacant seats. Mr W J Smith, of North Street, who for 30 years had gratuitously undertaken ministerial duties at the Church, had known him throughout that time and spoke of him as one of the best fathers and among the most truly Christian and self-sacrificing men he had ever known. For over 20 years, without a break, Mr Wood Snr, a hard-working shoemaker, saved £1/10- (£1.50) for the Sussex Home Missionary Society, besides contributing to other religious and philanthropic agencies. Mrs Wood, for her part, was equally highly spoken of by those who know her. She regularly attended Belgrave Street Church and took an active interest in its affairs. Mr Smith thought her a good woman and a good mother.

Wood Jnr followed the family tradition and was even at church on the Sunday before the murder. Evidently he was much liked among his relatives and friends, who were utterly astounded at the dreadful charge brought against him. Everyone who knew him gave him an excellent character, and those who worked with him regarded him as a straightforward and companionable man. *The Argus* was anxious he should not be condemned in advance:

His parents seem incapable of entertaining for a moment the idea that he can be guilty. If Wood is proved to be guilty and is proved also to be sane then nobody can possibly sympathise with him. Meanwhile he has not been tried and is entitled to be regarded as an innocent man.

But none of this carried much weight with the people of Brighton. Following the brief proceedings of his second appearance in the Police Court on 15 December, there was a remarkably hostile demonstration by the waiting crowd, as *The Argus* duly reported:

> *... contrary to the usual custom, the prisoner was not removed to Lewes Gaol quickly after the rising of the Court. Many of the crowd wearied of waiting but it was generally believed that Wood would be taken to Lewes during the day, and in the afternoon a large and increasing crowd gathered outside the entrance to the police station, on the western side of the Town Hall. No prison van, however, made its appearance. The police had decided upon a strategic movement and as soon as dusk closed in, the van was quietly taken into East Street and stationed in the square opposite Beal's.*
>
> *At a favourable moment, Wood, escorted by two stalwart constables and accompanied by the Chief Constable, Fire Superintendent Lacroix, Inspector Parker and several other officers, was hastily run up the steps leading from the Sanitary Office, on the eastern side of the Town Hall. But a crowd has many eyes, and hardly had the prisoner appeared in Bartholomews before a signal was given and the crowd came down from the western side of the Town Hall in a perfect avalanche. East-street at the time was crowded, the pavement being thronged and the road laden with vehicular traffic. Under such conditions it was impossible for the police to make much headway and the crowd had time to close around the unhappy man and his guard.*
>
> *Wood seemed in a state of mortal agony. The crowd near the man 'booed' and hissed him, while the main body in the rear set up a running fire of execration and abuse. Such cries as a 'You villain,' 'You hound,' 'Let's get at you' were heard, and oaths and curses were freely intermingled, the voices of women being as loud as any. The police flanked the man to prevent a rush being made, and the constables hurried forward, the prisoner seeming even more anxious to cover the distance than they were. On turning the corner off the square, Wood began to run, mounted the steps of the prison van without assistance and was lost to view in the twinkling of an eye. The crowd surged around the vehicle, and kept up a long yell. The horse, a powerful animal, became frightened at the demonstration, and began to back. This only excited the crowd the more, and they closed round shouting 'Over with it!', 'Turn it over!' 'Let's have him!'. The police managed to make a headway for the animal, which broke into a trot when the whip was applied, and started on its way to Lewes Gaol amid a continued chorus of execrations.*

The following day the people of Brighton, in much larger numbers, gave expression to feelings of an entirely different kind. The occasion was Edith Jeal's funeral.

In the morning, a vast but very orderly crowd, made up of the poorest people in one of the poorest parts of the town, gathered in Upper Bedford Street, the starting-point of the procession. The assembly waited patiently until the tiny polished oak coffin was brought out, covered in wreaths. All the women sobbed bitterly at the pathetic scene, a spectacle made still more heartrending when the distraught mother, leaning on her husband's arm, passed down Bedford Buildings to the mourning coach.

It took some time to arrange the numerous wreaths that had been sent. The little coffin was placed on an open conveyance drawn by a pair of horses and the floral tributes were placed on and around it. These came from strangers as well as friends, and included one from 'Edith's little school friends and teachers', a magnificent wreath from 'Sympathisers of the Market, Brighton' and others from the poor flower girls of Brighton.

The mourners, 21 in all, then took their places in four single-horse mourning coaches. The mother and father with two of their elder children occupied the first coach, the others being provided for in the remaining three.

It was just after twelve when the procession moved off, followed by the vast majority of the crowd. It passed down Upper Bedford Street into St James's Street. People were standing on the pavement along that busy thoroughfare, waiting to see the cortège pass. As in Upper Bedford Street, many of the shops had their shutters up. At the bottom of the street, on the Old Steine, was another large crowd. It was the same from that point until the Extra-Mural Cemetery was reached. While many of the people followed, others congregated at such spots as the fountain near St Peter's Church, the Level Police Station and at the bottom of Elm Grove.

There were crowds on both sides of Lewes Road, among them many children from neighbouring schools. It was a quarter to one when the slow cortège gradually approached the cemetery gates. Hundreds of the spectators filed in and wended their way up the long pathway between the tombs to the spot where the little body was to be laid.

The Argus reported:

> *... the air was hushed to silence and eyes that had been dry began to moisten with tears. The women wept, the men bowed their heads in reverence and the children clung to the gowns of their parents or huddled together in groups awe-struck and half in fear. The hard*

harsh monotone of the tolling bell has perhaps never before been echoed in so many human hearts. Every member of that vast varying crowd seemed affected, the sight conjuring up in appalling vividness the awful circumstances surrounding the little one's death.

The scene in the chapel was pitiful. Only the relatives and their near friends were admitted, the surging crowd being kept back by the police. The Reverend W T McCormick (Vicar of St Matthew's) conducted the service, assisted by his curate, the Reverend H H Bisshopp, who read the lesson. During the service, the bereaved mother's sobs could repeatedly be heard and the weeping faces of the children were distressing to witness. A large space around the grave was roped off and the crowd was kept back by a body of police under the charge of Inspector Parker and Fire Superintendent Lacroix. Near to the open grave a number of beautiful wreaths had been laid in readiness to be transferred onto the mound.

The remainder of the service at the grave was impressively read by the Reverend McCormick who, at the close, gave a short impromptu address. He would like, he said, to say a few words but he scarcely felt fit to do so under the circumstances. They had met there, a great body of mourners – mourning the loss of one God had taken to Himself. He had said 'Suffer little children to come unto Me, and forbid them not, for of such is the kingdom of Heaven'. He recommended them to do as the Apostles did when they lost their dear companion, go to Jesus Christ in their distress.

Many persons lingered behind after the mourners had left to look into the grave, and it was a long time before the sacred spot was left solely to the care of the gravedigger. The funeral arrangements had all been very capably handled by F J Reading of High Street.

Events moved rapidly forward. Three days after the burial, the adjourned/resumed inquest was held at Brighton Town Hall and three days after that, at the same place, the adjourned magistrates' hearing. Wood's final appearance at the Police Court was on 30 December 1891, when he was charged on remand with wilful murder.

Not until early April 1892 would the callous killer again be in the public eye, this time on the occasion of his trial at the Spring Assizes in Lewes.

The proceedings took place at County Hall on 7 April before Mr Justice Mathew. S H Day and W W Grantham appeared for the prosecution and C F Gill for the prisoner.

Wood appeared in the dock wearing a black coat, a stand-up collar with points turned down and a black tie. He appeared quite self-possessed and calm and in reply to the charge firmly answered 'Not

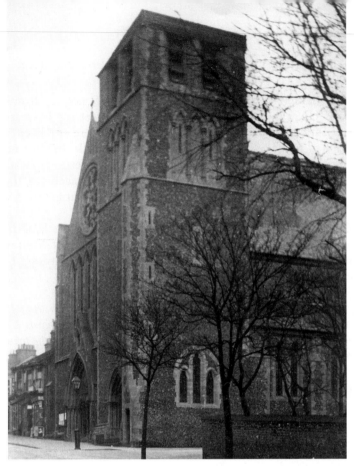

St Matthew's Church was erected in 1881–83 and stood at the corner of Sutherland Road and College Terrace. It was demolished in 1967 and the parish was merged with St Mark's. St Matthew's Court now stands on its site. Author's collection

Guilty'. He then took a seat in the centre of the dock as counsel for the prosecution rose to commence his opening statement.

Day outlined the crime and the case against Wood and summarised the testimony of the witnesses he would call. The evidence he produced could not be direct evidence, but circumstantial evidence. Apart from identification by a chain of people, there was the fact that Wood borrowed money from a fellow-employee in the Goods Department, Martin Marchant, to take a bath – doubtless to remove traces of his guilt. Then there was the point that Wood knew of the murder, and where it had been committed, scarcely before any reference to it had appeared in the newspapers. He had commented on it to goods carman, John Scrase. There was the physical evidence of bloodstains on the prisoner's clothing, then his patent lie of having been at the circus and his denial of knowing and seeing an old acquaintance, PC Tuppen.

The sightings formed a chain in which not a link seemed to be missing. After leaving the goods yard, Wood was first seen by a witness named Eliza Dunk in Sydney Street, not far from the station. He was then sighted in Edward Street by 11-year-old Fanny Pimm. Wood whistled to her, asked where she lived, and asked her to go with him. She refused. A little further along Edward Street, he was seen by 7-year-old Alice West, who was too young to be examined (her head did not quite reach the top of the witness box). Wood then exchanged a goodnight greeting with PC Tuppen at the bottom of Lavender Street.

Key testimony was provided by one Rose Leggatt. Wood, the worse for drink, fell up against her on the corner of Montague Street and Upper Bedford Street. She actually witnessed the moment of abduction:

> *I saw the man dressed in railway uniform. The man in the dock is the same. When I saw him he was putting his hand towards a little child outside Trengrove's shop, and I saw the child follow the prisoner to the middle of Somerset-street.*

In Somerset Street, Wood was sighted by a woman named Alice Guy, still going in the direction of the murder scene:

> *I saw a man on the opposite side of the road carrying a child, which was crying. I could not say the age of the child, but it seemed a large child. She had on a hat like the one produced. I called out to the man 'Don't hurt that poor little thing.' He turned round. He was under a lamp at the time he turned. I could see his face distinctly. He went towards the east and I followed him to the corner of Somerset-street. When he got to Egremont-place, he crossed the road, turned to the right and went towards the Hospital. Prisoner is the man I saw that night.*

Mrs Guy became hysterical on leaving the box and had to be assisted out of court.

At the top of Chesham Street, Henry Spicer, a printer, who was walking westward along Eastern Road, saw a man carrying a child and passed him at just about ten minutes to nine. The man, who was 'very tipsy', was going eastward and was about 150 yards from the field. His face was hidden in the child's clothes.

The task of Gill for the defence was well-nigh impossible, especially after Day made Wood Snr admit that his son had been convicted for horse stealing in Canada. Yet he valiantly did what he could on the prisoner's behalf. He warned the jury to be careful in dealing with evidence which was circumstantial, and pointed to the sheer violence of the crime as tending to show it had been committed by a someone insane. He appealed to the jury to take this view in the interests of common humanity. He also drew attention to the good character given to the prisoner and to the part played by drink in his downfall. Drink combined with his long-standing epilepsy would be liable to result in epileptic seizures. Gill called medical evidence as to his condition, not in a bid for him to be set free but so that 'he should be confined with others who had committed offences while insane and live a life of seclusion.'

Dr C E Saunders, Medical Superintendent of the Sussex County Lunatic Asylum, said he had had special experience in insanity. He had made epilepsy a study and currently had at least 100 patients. He had been instructed by the Treasury to see the prisoner and had done so twice. He was then perfectly rational. That was not inconsistent with his being an epileptic. Saunders was examined at length as to the effects epilepsy had on patients and he pointed out that drink or lust would be likely to bring on an attack. Perennial insanity was shown by statistics to take place most usually in middle life. Epilepsy and insanity were closely allied.

Dr Sheppard, another lunacy specialist, had also visited the prisoner. He said that epileptics leading a dissolute life were sometimes inclined to acts of violence and epileptics should be very cautious as to their mode of living.

Judge Mathew, in his lengthy summing-up, gave short shrift to any notion of irresponsibility on the part of the accused. As to Wood's apparent amnesia about the crime, he pointed to his claiming to have been at the circus rather than saying he had no recollection of the evening before. He also felt that it was 'idle to talk of uncontrollable impulse' and that epilepsy could not

This view along Chesham Road shows Rock Street, its eastward extension, in the distance. Wood lived at No 11, on the left-hand side near the end of the street. The property has survived. Author's collection

account for unconsciousness of action ('Was he unconscious when carrying the child through the street?'). Nor was the atrocity of crime any defence, for 'atrocious crimes are committed by people who know perfectly well what they are doing.'

The jury, after an absence of eight minutes, returned a verdict of Guilty and Wood was sentenced to death. He was removed from the dock in a state of near-collapse.

★ ★ ★

To add to the frustration of the defence, certain items of evidence were deemed inadmissible during the trial since they were not made on oath. These were the reports into Wood's mental state by Dr Saunders and Dr Sheppard, each expert producing one each, and letters from the Manitoba Penitentiary – now Stony Mountain Institution – referring to Wood's health and conduct during his detention in that place. It was a maximum-security institution, administered by a strict regime, located 15 miles north of Winnipeg. On 23 August 1886, at Portage la Prairie, Manitoba, Wood had been sentenced to serve three years and 10 months in Stony Mountain for stealing. He was discharged on 4 November 1889, returning direct to England through his father assisting in his passage home.

Saunders reported there was at present no evidence of mental derangement but abundant evidence to prove that Wood had repeated attacks of epilepsy while in Canada. He went so far as to state:

> *Granting the fact that the man is epileptic, his irresponsibility for the deed he committed may be strongly affirmed.*

His disregard of the consequences of his crime was revealed by the entire absence of any apparent attempt to conceal the body of the child. Saunders observed that rape was not a common crime among epileptics but it still found a place in the statistics and he concurred with another expert in concluding that epileptics could not be held responsible for any act of violence perpetrated during their unconscious automatism, which they had no power to control, nor capacity to judge.

Dr Sheppard's report ran broadly along the same lines.

In drawing up their reports, both doctors made use of letters from Canada. There were six of these, all written between 12 February and 17 February 1892. From them, it emerged that Wood spent no less than 49 days in hospital and was convalescing and unfit for duty (i.e. hard labour) for a further 84 on account

The Manitoba Penitentiary, now Stony Mountain Institution, near Winnipeg, where Wood served nearly four years for stealing. Correctional Service, Canada

of his condition; that he was well behaved and received all the remission of time it was possible for him to obtain; and that he was a communicant of the Church of England. A jailer, William Moss, did point out that prior to his August 1886 sentence, Wood had previously served time on two occasions, once for seven days and once for three months. On his behalf, however, he stated 'I consider him a character not responsible for any of his actions.'

Written support for Wood's reprieve was expressed in a petition to the Crown and in letters from one correspondent in particular to the *Sussex Daily News*.

The petition was got up by relatives and friends of the condemned man, especially his father. It prayed the Home Secretary to advise the Queen to commute the capital sentence to one of detention in a criminal lunatic asylum during Her Majesty's pleasure. Sent with it were the letters from Canada, the reports by Drs Saunders and Sheppard and a verbatim report of the trial. Despite the several hundred signatories including nearly twenty leading medical practitioners and many clergymen and solicitors in Brighton and district, the Home Secretary rejected the petition.

The *Sussex Daily News* was the medium for a writer styling himself 'Humanitas' to plead Wood's cause. He had signed the petition and wanted to make a stand against 'the brutalising lust for a fellow-creature's blood.' He argued that as not one man in probably ten million, or many more, had ever had the slightest desire to murder and mutilate children, a deterrent could scarcely be required; that the evidence of the highest available authorities on mental disease was distinctly in favour of the irresponsibility of the accused; and that the slaughter of a fellow-mortal in cold blood was anti-Christian (despite the clergy reading the Burial Office over his living body).

'Humanitas' had violent critics, especially 'Sanitas', who accused him of sentimentality. Both were rounded on by 'Justice', who declined to join in the former's hysterical scream for what the writer contended would be a gross miscarriage of justice. 'Humanitas' later complained of the personal animosity against himself from various correspondents. 'Barrister' wondered why Wood's workmates did not support him if they believed him to be a confirmed epileptic. 'G.E.' wrote that the question whether epilepsy was a disease which rendered a person irresponsible for his actions was purely and solely a medical question and ought to be left to medical men to decide:

> *We do not consult lawyers on medical matters any more than we consult medical men on questions of law.*

A 'Worthing Mother' wrote expressing surprise at the people of Brighton signing a petition in favour of the commutation of the death sentence. The verdict was, she says, right and just, and if ever a man deserved hanging, Wood did. Her sentiments, and those of the majority of the population, were echoed by 'Fairplay', who found fault with the medical men showing what he termed 'ill-advised sympathy and theoretical excuses for the monster Wood.' He added:

> *It seems hard to understand the sickly sentimentality for this monster from a body of men who are not as a rule given to sentiment. I trust that some of the medical men in Brighton, possessing manhood and humanity, will come forward and protest against this unhappy wretch escaping the penalty of his crime.*

The law duly took its course.

On the eve of his execution, Wood was visited by his father and two sisters. He bore up very well during the interview but their final parting was very painful. Shortly after they left he was seized with an epileptic fit, during which he foamed at the mouth and had to be held down. Later in the evening, Mr Wilkinson, Congregational Minister of Lewes, came and found him very shaky and no longer calm. Wood took the minister's hand and pleaded with him not to leave him but to be with him to the end. Mr Wilkinson consented.

Asked if he had anything to acknowledge, Wood replied in heartbroken tones:

> *I'm sorry for what I did. I wish my sincere sorrow to be conveyed to the parents of the child for the great wrong I have done; but I have no recollection whatever about it.*

He also dictated three messages for the minister to pass to the press for publication. The first was to the parents of the child praying for their forgiveness, the second was to his fellow-workmen at the railway who had conveyed their support and the third was to his defence team, to Mr W J Smith (the Minister of Belgrave Street Chapel) and to Mr Wilkinson, thanking them all for their kindness and the efforts they had made on his behalf. He also wrote a long letter to his parents the next morning.

He passed a fairly good night, but ate and drank little from the coffee, bread, butter and egg supplied for his breakfast. He was calm and prayerful at first, although he became nervous and depressed as the gallows loomed. Again he appealed to the minister to be with him to the end, and just before Billington, the executioner, entered the cell he went on his knees in earnest prayer, a prayer in which he again, and for the last time, stated that God knew he did not recollect anything about the crime for which he was about to die.

The small group comprising the prisoner, governor, surgeon, executioner and others entered the cell and without a moment's hesitation Billington pinioned Wood at the elbows. The procession moved off and when the burial service was read, the mournful toll of the chapel bell could be heard.

Wood appeared to walk firmly and with head erect, until the awful moment when he saw the scaffold. This had been put up at the south-east corner of the prison precints, close to where the road from Brighton to Chailey turned off. His face became deathly pale and he seemed to turn an appealing glance at three reporters stationed on the green sward a short distance away. Yet he never faltered and went straight on to meet his fate. He did not flinch and seemed firm to the last. Billington went about his work swiftly and in a businesslike manner. Death was, without any doubt, instantaneous. There was no swaying of the rope, nor could the slightest movement be discerned down in the pit. The white cap had slipped on one side and it could be seen that Wood's eyes were closed, and the face somewhat distorted, while on the right side there was a slight abrasion. The signal that the execution had been carried out was passed from one warder to another until it reached the man stationed over the main entrance, who immediately hoisted the black flag as evidence to those outside that justice had been served.

On the day George Henry Wood was hanged, the air was heavy with the scents and sounds of springtime. In the bright sunshine, the gardens and paths of Bedford Buildings no doubt resounded to the shouts of playing children – children who might, from time to time, affectionately remember the games and laughter they once enjoyed with their little companion, Edith Jeal.

Bibliography

BOOKS

Anon. *History of the Brighton Police 1838–1967*, ESRO Ref. SP43/10/4

Bardens, Dennis *Famous Cases of Norman Birkett KC*, London, Robert Hale Ltd, 1963

Beevers, David & Roles, John *A Pictorial History of Brighton*, Derby, The Breedon Books Publishing Company Limited, 1993

Blaker, Nathaniel Paine, MRCS *Reminiscences of Nathaniel Paine Blaker*, first published in 1906 for private circulation only. New edition, revised, extended and largely rewritten, published by Combridges of Hove, December 1919, under the title *Sussex in Bygone Days.*

Brent, C & Rector, W *Victorian Lewes*, Chichester, Phillimore & Co Ltd, 1980

Brent, Colin *Historic Lewes and its Buildings*, Lewes, Town Council Official Guide, 1995

Briffett, David *Sussex Murders*, Southampton, Ensign Publications, 1990

Browne, Douglas G & Tullett, E V *Bernard Spilsbury – His Life and Cases*, London, Geo. G Harrap & Co Ltd, 1951

Canning, John (Ed.) *Unsolved Murders and Mysteries*, London, Futura Publications, 1988

Carder, Timothy *The Encyclopaedia of Brighton*, East Sussex County Libraries, 1990

Dale, Antony *Brighton Town and Brighton People*, Chichester, Phillimore & Co. Ltd., 1976

Eddleston, John J *Murderous Sussex – The Executed of the Twentieth Century*, Derby, The Breedon Books Publishing Company Limited, 1997

Farrant, Sue *Georgian Brighton, 1740–1820*, University of Sussex, 1980

Fielding, Steve *The Hangman's Record, Volume 1, 1868–1899*, Beckenham, Chancery House Press, 1994

Fielding, Steve *The Hangman's Record, Volume 2, 1900–1929*, Beckenham, Chancery House Press, 1995

Folthorp, Robert *Folthorp's Brighton Directory*, Brighton [Various dates]

Harrison, Frederick & North, James Sharp *Old Brighton, Old Hove, Old Preston*, Hassocks, Flare Books, 1937, reprinted 1974

Hawkings, David T *Criminal Ancestors – A Guide to Historical Criminal Records in England and Wales*, Stroud, Alan Sutton Publishing Ltd, 1992

Hill, Rocky *Underdog Brighton: A Rather Different History of the Town*, Brighton, Iconoclast Press, 1991

Hindley, Charles (Ed.) *The Brighton Murder, An Authentic and Faithful History of the Atrocious Murder of Celia Holloway ...etc.*, Brighton, 1875.

Holter, Graham *Sussex Breweries*, Seaford, SB Publications, 2001

Horlock, Christopher *Brighton & Hove Then and Now – Volume II*, Seaford, S B Publications, 2003

Jenks, G S 'On the Sanitary Condition of Brighton 1840', (see The Chadwick Report), BPP, 1842

Johnson, W H *Sussex Tales of Mystery and Murder*, Newbury, Countryside Books, 2002

Johnson, W H *Brighton's First Trunk Murderer, 1831*, Downsway Books, Eastbourne, 1995

Johnson, W H *Sussex Villains*, Newbury, Countryside Books, 2003

Knowles, Leonard *Court of Drama – Famous Trials at Lewes Assizes*, London, John Long Ltd, 1966

Lustgarten, Edgar *Defender's Triumph*, London, Pan Books Ltd, 1951

Middleton, Judy *Encyclopaedia of Hove and Portslade*, Portslade, 2001–2003

Musgrave, Clifford *Life in Brighton*, Rochester, Rochester Press, 1981

Page, Thomas *Page's Brighton Directory*, Brighton [Various dates]

Pike *Pike's Brighton Directory* [various dates]

Poole, Helen *Lewes Past*, Chichester, Phillimore & Co Ltd, 2000

Rowland, David *The Brighton Blitz*, Seaford, SB Publications, 1997

Sellwood, Arthur and Mary *The Victorian Railway Murders*, Newton Abbot, David & Charles, 1979

Sparrow, Gerald *Women Who Murder*, Arthur Barker Ltd, London, 1970 [untrustworthy as a source for the Edmunds case]

Taylor, Rupert *Sussex Murder Casebook*, Newbury, Countryside Books, 1994

Towner, William J *Towner's Brighton Directory* [various dates]

Tullett, Tom *Clues to Murder*, London, The Bodley Head, 1986

Various contributors *Backyard Brighton – Photographs and Memories of Brighton in the Thirties*, Brighton Queenspark Book No 20, 1988

Various contributors *Back Street Brighton – Photographs and Memories*, Brighton Queenspark Book No 22 and Lewis Cohen Urban Studies Centre, Brighton Polytechnic, nd. [ca. 1993]

Windrum, Anthony *Horsham – An Historical Survey*, Chichester, Phillimore & Co Ltd, 1978

Wojtczak, Helen *Women of Victorian Sussex*, Hastings, The Hastings Press, 2003

Wright, Charles *The Brighton Ambulator*, Print of Donaldson's Library, 1818. Hine's Office, (52 East Street, Brighton')

NEWSPAPERS, PERIODICALS AND MISCELLANEOUS DOCUMENTS

Annual Register, The 'The Brighton Poisoning Case', *Remarkable Trials* Series, pp. 189–201, Rivingtons, 1873

Argus/Evening Argus Various dates & Centenary Supplement, 31.3.1980 Murders Supplement, various dates, 1998

Brighton Gazette Various dates

Brighton Guardian Various dates

Brighton Herald Various dates

Mapleton, Percy Lefroy Unpublished MS, PRO HO 144/83 A6404

Real-Life Crimes (partwork) *The Brighton Trunk Murders*, Vol. 3, Part 39, London, Eaglemoss Publications Ltd, 1993

Sussex Advertiser, Surrey Gazette, etc. 13 February 1849

Sussex County Magazine 'The Newtimber Murder Mystery', Ackerman, Lewis T, Vol. 26 (8), August 1952, pp 387–388

Sussex County Magazine 'The Sussex County Gaol at Horsham', Albery, William, Vol. 6 (12), December 1932, pp 804–810

Sussex County Magazine 'A Downland Mystery', Beckett, Arthur, Vol. 6(4), April 1932, pp 255–257

Sussex Daily News Various dates

Sussex Express Various dates

Sussex Industrial History Issues 22 ('Seven Brighton Brewers' by Peter Holtham) and 26 ('The Sea House Hotel' by Geoffrey Mead)

Sussex Yesterdays No 2, pp. 39–43, 'Recollections of Horsham and Henry Burstow.'

Index